NOSTALGIA SPOTLIGHT ON THE FORTIES

UNION JACK

Wednesday, September 13, 1944
No. 80   Two Lire

FOR THE BRITISH FIGHTING FORCES

STOP PRESS

GERMANS USING EVERY FORM TRANSPORT FOR COMPLETE EVACUATION FROM ALSACE OF CIVILIANS, MACHINES, STORES, SAYS ZURICH REPORT. POLITICAL PRISONERS TAKEN TO GERMANY.

INTO GERMANY

Smashing across Luxembourg in two days, American troops have driven into Germany in force and are fighting five to ten miles inside the frontier. The penetration was made by General Hodges' First Army. This has advanced to the fortress of Trier in the heart of the Siegfried Line.

Blasted out of the sky

As Eisenhower's men began their drive into the R e i c h the Luftwaffe's precious fighter reserves, kept out of D-day action to defend the Fatherland, were forced up to meet 1,800 American planes raiding desperately needed German synthetic oil plants.

A hundred and seventy-five German planes were destroyed, bringing losses to 300 in two days.

Full story in Page 3.

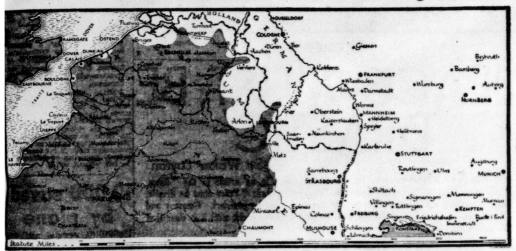

Russians top Carpathians

TO-DAY the Soviet Army stands on the threshold of the plains of Hungary.

German reports say that a Russian tank army has stormed the 9,000ft. main ridge of the Transylvania Alps and holds one of the highest passes. The entrance to Central Europe and the great plain stretching from Transylvania across Hungary lies before the Soviet armour.

The Soviet communique claims the capture of Sighisoaro and Medias, 30 miles north of captured Sibiu in central Rumania, and Petroseni, 50 miles south-west of Sibiu.

The Germans have admitted the evacuation of Krosno, 45 miles west of Przemysl and 17 miles from the northern border of Czechoslovakia, but no claim of its capture has been made by Moscow.

The Russians have made some local gains north-east of Warsaw on the Lomza front.

Patrols continue to harass the Germans across the Lithuanian-Prussian border.

North-South link — Official

OTHER great news from France yesterday was: General Patton's First Army has opened an offensive along a 50-mile front to force the Moselle River defences; British patrols are ranging across the Dutch border following an armoured break-through across the Escaut Canal; it was officially announced that units of the First Army have joined with patrols of the Seventh driving up from the south; French troops have captured Dijon; the Le Havre garrison is reported to have surrendered to British troops.

— And by the way

The news an expectant world has been waiting for hourly was announced at SHAEF early yesterday morning.

But not by General Eisenhower, or Field-Marshal Montgomery, or even by a "high-ranking Allied officer." The great moment was given to a briefing officer—and he gave the news casually at the tail end of his summary of the fighting.

He had worked his way from Antwerp to the southern flank of the 1st Army. Then, without the slightest trace of emphasis upon the importance of his words, he said: "General Hodges' Army, after an artillery bombardment, have edged their way across the Siegfried Line and have penetrated this fortress chain to a depth of five miles, reaching a point in the vicinity of Trier."

Stalin was invited

MARSHAL STALIN received an invitation to the conference between Mr. Churchill and President Roosevelt, but declined on the grounds that he could not leave Russia when such big battles were proceeding, it is reported from Quebec.

Churchill and Roosevelt continued their discussions in the Chateau Frontenac far into the night on Monday and resumed them again early yesterday. Plans for the coming all-out offensive against Japan were considered, says Reuter's correspondent.

The President's secretary, Stephen Early, said yesterday that the talks will be almost exclusively of a military nature.

Early reports of the fighting on German soil said that General Hodges' army was meeting with "a fair amount" of resistance. A few hours prior to the announcement, German radio stations were reporting that troops were massing and that our guns were laying down a heavy bombardment. "They have obviously been ordered to crash eastward," the announcers declared.

Diagram maps of the area show a line of Siegfried fortifications running west of Trier. These have been overcome. To the east runs another line, and this is being assaulted.

A few days ago General Guderian, Germany's tank expert, boasted that Allied soldiers would never set foot on German soil.

Front-line reports yesterday said that General Patton's army has launched an assault to force the Moselle along a 50-mile front. Resistance along the whole length is stubborn and several counter-attacks have been made.

South of Metz a bridgehead was lost early in the battle, but infantry, tanks and tank destroyers forced another crossing a mile away. The battle is still raging.

A few miles to the north, other Third Army forces have captured a mile length of the Maginot Line along the Luxembourg frontier. The line, and the fortress of Aumetz, is intact and the huge electrically-operated guns are in working order. There is no evidence that the Germans tried to turn the guns round or prepare the line against invasion.

British patrols have crossed the frontier into Holland and are probing defences south of Eindhoven. This advance followed a tank break-through from the Bourg Leopold bridgehead. Little German armour appeared to oppose the thrust, but enemy infantry was very active with tank destroying weapons, says Reuter. The Escaut Canal was crossed in this area after a battle in which several German guns were smashed and heavy casualties inflicted on the infantry.

"More Germans were killed and more of their equipment smashed on Monday than in the whole 200-mile run to Brussels," says a Reuter correspondent. "The main battle was for a cluster of fortified houses at a crossroads just short of the canal. We captured it and rushed a bridge before the defenders had time to set off the explosive charges to blow it."

The whole of the battalion charged with defending the area was wiped out.

The bridgehead is now firmly held, though the enemy has attacked it several times with spandaus and nebelwerfers.

Greatly increased resistance is reported from all other sectors of the Albert Canal area. No gains were made on Monday. General Dempsey's men are massing for a major blow, correspondents report, and at the moment we are content to batter the German defences with our artillery.

General Eisenhower met Field-Marshal Montgomery in Brussels on Monday to confer with him and other commanders, says Reuter.

Reports that the garrison at Le Havre surrendered yesterday are unconfirmed, although latest messages say we hold three-quarters of the port. Earlier in the day Canadian troops were reported to be closing in through heavy mortar and machine-gun fire after one assault had been thrown back.

British troops joined the siege on Sunday, battling through the Foret de Mongeon into the northern suburbs of the port.

The whole stretch of coast for a distance of 55 miles between Gravelines and Zeebrugge has now been cleared with the excep-

(TURN TO PAGE FOUR)

NO REICH-SWISS RAIL TRAFFIC

Railway traffic between Germany and Switzerland is virtually suspended, says the Swiss radio. Trains arriving from Germany show shell holes and other damage.—*Reuter.*

NOT WANTED

The Turkish Government has decided to refuse admission to Axis military and civil refugees from Axis countries or from the Aegean and Mediterranean islands.—*Reuter.*

FIFTH NOW REACH GOTHIC LINE

BRITISH and American troops have now penetrated between two and three miles into the high ground across the Upper Sieve River, and both the Fifth and Eighth Armies are in contact with Gothic Line positions in many places along the entire front.

Heavy fighting continues on the Adriatic sector, where British troops are now firmly established west of Gemmano. Bitter fighting has been going on for the high feature known as Point 449, just to the east of Gemmano, and a foothold has been gained.

Since the start of the battle on this front—on August 26—3,500 prisoners have been taken by the 8th Army.

In the central sector, 8th Army troops have established themselves without opposition on

Monte Falucchio, a 2,750ft. feature in the mountains between the Upper Tiber and Arno Rivers.

Considerable advances were reported along the entire front, and our patrols have penetrated several forward positions of the Gothic Line and hold the high ground in the vicinity of Barberino. This is the northernmost point in Italy now in Allied hands.

Indian troops, after an advance of two-and-a-half miles, have established a bridgehead across the Sieve, south of Vicchio. Farther west we are across the river in some strength to a depth of about two miles.

North of Florence the greatest advances of the period were made. Positions have been captured three miles beyond the

Sieve, in the vicinity of Scarperia. Fifth Army units to the west are keeping abreast of this advance, and most of the high ground in the Monte della Calvana mass is in our hands. Patrols are fanning out from Pistola, while others have forced their way over the Massa Cozzile.

Fifth Army elements are firmly established across the Serchio river, three miles north of Lucca and are continuing their drive to the north.

It was announced yesterday that units of the Royal Navy are bombarding the east coast of Italy in support of the Army in the Rimini area. Results were reported as excellent. There was return fire from the shore, but our ships suffered neither damage nor casualties.

NOSTALGIA SPOTLIGHT ON THE FORTIES

Michael Anglo

First published in 1977 by
JUPITER BOOKS (LONDON) LIMITED
167 Hermitage Road, London N4 1LZ.

Copyright © Jupiter Books (London) Limited 1977

SBN 904041 55 7

This edition produced in 1985 by
Universal Books Ltd.,
The Grange,
Grange Yard,
London SE1 3AG

Composed in Photon Baskerville and
printed and bound in Great Britain by
R. J. Acford, Industrial Estate, Chichester.

Contents

Let 'em all come

IN JULY 1940, OUR BATTALION WAS STATIONED ON THE SOUTH Coast a few miles east of Dover. We were billeted in the Duke of York's Royal Military School (D.Y.R.M.S.), an extensive camp consisting of dormitory and domestic buildings, a large central building serving as a mess with a tower used as an observation post, parade grounds, and a number of ancillary hutments built by soldiers. There was also a large, galleried gymnasium which the Provost used as quarters, the changing rooms serving as detention cells. Under the same roof was a swimming bath.

The former inmates of the school had been the young sons of soldiers, now evacuated to safer areas. All they had left behind were wire beds no more than five feet long, a bit too short for the comfort of an average soldier. In the ablutions, washbasins, showers, and lavatory pans were low, having been built for boy soldiers who wore short trousers as part of their khaki uniform.

We thought the bungalows a vast improvement on our old billets, which had been in tents, stables, and disused houses, but before long we found that much of our time had to be spent on outpost duties, manning trenches and dug-outs, pill-boxes, road blocks, and derelict cliff-top cottages near Dover at places such as Guston and Swingate, all along the coast to St. Margaret's Bay.

Within the camp each bungalow block was sandbagged, and sentries were posted nightly at each block all the way from the main gate on the Dover road to the Guston Gate at the rear of the camp. Platoons from our regiment and others returning to camp for forty-eight hours "rest" after periods on outpost duty had to provide the guard.

Strung out along the coast road between the D.Y.R.M.S. and Dover there were other military establishments, and most received daily droppings from German aircraft and an occasional shell or two lobbed over from the German coastal batteries across the Channel.

One day our section took over a post from the Queen's Westminsters, consisting of a short trench system with a bren-gun emplacement. We were billeted in an isolated block of four decrepit terrace cottages on the cliff top not far from the radiolocation masts, which received a good deal of attention from the Germans from time to time. There was a gully leading down to the beach, which had been blocked with rolls of barbed wire.

Our duty, in case of a German landing, was to defend the gully. There were eleven of us in our section, and we had our rifles, a bren-gun, and ten Molotov cocktails left behind by the Queen's Westminsters, with which to do the job. We drew rations daily, foraging for extras and doing most of our own cooking as well as brewing up every time we thought of it, which was often. We therefore needed plenty of fuel. So apparently had our predecessors. They had already used all the bannisters and every other step of the staircase for that purpose. We were hard pressed to find fuel for ourselves. We took up the odd floorboard, then more of the stairs, which made mounting to the next floor a precarious business. In order to start fires, lacking paper and kindling, we hit upon the splendid idea of using the contents of the Molotov cocktails. These were old wine bottles filled with an inflammable concoction consisting mainly, I believe, of a petrol and resin mixture. Attached to the neck of the bottle by a wire was a piece of cotton waste or "four-by-two". The idea was that one soaked the waste in some of the inflammable liquid, lit it, then hurled the bottle at a tank in the hope that the tank would "brew up" and be put out of action. As fuel for our fires Molotov cocktails were very successful, and every time we emptied a bottle of its contents we refilled it by peeing into it. Finally we were left with ten bottles of pee, which did not worry us too much.

Then one night the order came to "stand to". We had already "stood to" at dusk, so we wondered what it was all about. A little while later our platoon officer rattled up the road on his bicycle and told us that this was it. A German landing was expected to take place that night, and good luck. After he had gone off to another section, posted around a house further down the road, the corporal told me and my "mucker" Dicky Dormer, a tall, gangling Fusilier whose trousers were forever creeping up above his gaiters, that our job was to go down into the gully outside the wire taking the Molotovs with us, hide in some bushes, and wait to deal with anything or anybody that tried to get up the gully from the beach.

"Right! What are you waiting for? Move off, and make it *jaldi*," said the corporal.

Dicky eyed the corporal distastefully. "I suppose you know what's in these bottles," he said. "Some of it is yours, y'know."

"I know," said the corporal, "but that's your hard luck. We've got our orders. Any sign of the Jerries, chuck the bottles and scramble back up here fast. If you're lucky we'll open a gap in the wire for you."

The rest of the section thought the situation was highly hilarious and was breaking up with laughter. One squaddy suggested that our best chance was to offer the Germans a drink and poison them. Dicky said very funny and how would he like a bottle rammed down his throat for a start?

Preparing for war: men of the Tank Corps parade in their new battledress.

Dicky and I made ourselves comfortable in the gully using the case of Molotovs as a back-rest and settled down for a crafty smoke.

"Christ!" I said. "We're going to stop the German Army with ten bottles of piss."

"The Germans won't come," said Dicky confidently; "but if they do, wake me up. I'm going to have a kip."

"I'll give you an hour," I said, "then it's my turn."

The Germans did not come. The next morning as it was growing light we hurled the bottles into the sea and clambered back up the cliff and through a gap in the barbed wire which Dicky had thoughtfully left open just in case the corporal might have forgotten his promise. Nobody noticed the Molotovs were missing, and when the Queen's Westminsters took over a day or two later, their corporal did not even mention them. But the next time we manned the post we found a case of Mills bombs in one of the rooms. "What's the use of them?" said Dicky. "You can't use *them* for cooking."

One night Dicky and I were on sentry duty outside one of the bungalows in the D.Y.R.M.S. where our platoon was billeted. A guard consisted of six men, providing sentries on a roster of two hours on "stag" and four hours off. Dicky and I were on our second "stag". I was at the front entrance to the bungalow, Dicky was at the rear. Every so often we were supposed to check with each other.

After a few minutes Dicky wandered around to where I was leaning against the sandbags and said, "No sense in the two of us hanging about like a pair of old cobblers. I'll nip in for a kip for an hour, then I'll relieve you so you can have a kip. If you challenge

9

anyone do it nice and loud and I'll be out like a streak of duck's shit, so don't worry."

"All right," I said, "but don't take off your bloody boots as you usually do. If the orderly officer or sergeant come nosing around, you'll never get them on in time."

Actually the idea was that whenever a sentry challenged anybody the other sentry would quickly move round the bungalow and cover his partner from the shadows. Anybody coming through the main gate at night would be challenged loudly by sentries outside bungalows and stores every fifty yards along the main road through camp, and we would brace ourselves ready for the ritual. "Halt! Who goes there?" The person challenged was supposed to halt in his tracks and shout, "Friend!" Whereupon the sentry would yell back, "Advance, friend, and be recognized." If it was someone he had already recognized he would more often than not yell, "Advance and be sterilized," or "Advance and be paralysed."

After midnight, on this occasion, all was quiet except for the sound of some activity on the other side of the Channel. I had a cigarette in my cupped hand when I thought I heard movement near an air raid shelter between our bungalow and one further down the road. The fag went into my pocket.

I thought it might be a dog on the prowl. I saw someone move in the shadows by the ablutions close to our bungalow. Orderly sergeant? Orderly officer? Where's Dormer? Right! A challenge! A nice loud one. Wake the whole bloody camp. Some hopes. Nobody turned out even when bombs dropped.

"Halt!" I yelled at the top of my voice. "Who goes there?"

No reply. I waited a few seconds. No Dormer. No movement.

"Halt!" I yelled again. "Who goes there?"

No reply, and now I was sure someone was lurking in the shadows close to our bungalow. Where's Dormer? If it's the orderly officer our Dicky is going to be on a "Fizzer" for sure. Then I saw a silhouette and I could see it was not Dormer.

I raised my bayoneted rifle. I already had a round up the spout. "Halt," I bellowed, "or I'll fire!" I was not joking. I thought, If it is someone playing silly buggers I'll give him the old "Tom tits" and wake up Dormer and the rest of the platoon at the same time, perhaps.

"Friend! Friend!" called the figure, belatedly, coming out onto the roadway.

"Advance, friend, and be recognized!" I continued the ritual.

An officer stepped forward. It was nobody I knew. He was an earnest-looking young man wearing a forage cap in the centre of his head with his hair spiking out from under it in all directions. His trousers were pulled up high above his gaiters. He looked like a rookie or . . . no! Surely not an imposter. I asked him to identify himself.

"I'm in charge of Nine Platoon, A Company," he said. "Where's the other sentry?" Nine Platoon was my platoon. But this officer was a stranger. Was this some sort of scheme by some half-witted commanding officer to test security at the camp? A dangerous one for the testing officer, to be sure. The officer proffered his identification.

11

Planning the invasion of
Britain: Hitler and Admiral
Raeder in May 1940.

12

Nobody had ever bothered to show us what such identification consisted of before, so I kept my bayonet pointing at his chest.

"Where's the other sentry?" he demanded again.

"Right here," said a voice from the shadows, "and I've got you covered. If you don't want a bayonet up your arse, stand still." Dormer had arrived.

"Very good," said the officer, grinning. "Very good indeed. I'm Mr. Wyatt, your platoon officer. I only arrived today. I'm sorry we haven't met before."

By this time our corporal and the rest of the guard had turned out, and the corporal was able to identify the officer, whose name was Woodrow Wyatt. Our new commander asked us if we had had enough food. Naturally we said we had not and were indeed very hungry. He opened his valise and brought out a load of sandwiches, then he said good night and departed.

"No sense in putting on my boots now," said Dormer.

Towards the end of October (or was it November?) I was out with the Intelligence Section on our newly issued heavy green-painted bikes, ostensibly on a "recce". We were teetering one behind the other down a country lane somewhere between Lyminge and Elham when we were amazed to see a rider come galloping round the bend. It was an officer, complete with corduroy riding breeches and shiny tan riding boots. He waved us down, urgently yelling for us to get off the road, and jockeying his horse back and forth he forced us into a ditch. There we waited expectantly. For what? Cavalry? In this war, very likely. Bren-carriers? Possibly. There had been rumours that some units had received one or two. Tanks? What hopes.

Then we gasped with astonishment as a group of supercilious riders in hunting pink came cantering past with barking hounds leaping along at the horses' hooves. We shouted "Tally-ho" and gave them a ripe royal raspberry as they disappeared down the road, then, swearing, we pulled our bikes from the ditch and stood squelching in our boots by the side of the road.

"Would you Adam and Eve it?" exploded our red-faced sergeant. "I thought there was a bloody war on." He added a few more remarks, robust and rude.

"Oh, I dunno," said our lance-jack, who was from Glasgow. "If Jerry comes maybe the sight of that little lot will scare the living daylights out of them. Perhaps they're some sort of secret weapon. Maybe bren-guns pop out of the horses' arseholes. Maybe . . ." He elaborated, and so did the rest of us.

The sergeant shook his head in disgust. "There's a teashop in Elham," he said. "We'll nip along there sharpish, and after that we'll poodle off to some quiet field for a 'laugh and a joke' and a little 'snore' until it's time for the NAAFI to open." Again he shook his head. "Hunting bloody foxes!" he said. "Some people don't know there's a bloody war on."

Soon after the evacuation of the shattered British Army from

Dunkirk, the Prime Minister was asked in Parliament whether he would issue an order that, in the event of an attack on this country, all orders given on the wireless to cease fire or lay down arms should automatically be disregarded by the fighting services.

The Lord Privy Seal, Clement Attlee, replied that appropriate measures were being taken to deal with enemy interference of the kind suggested, but, he added, it seemed inconceivable to him that members of His Majesty's Forces should even assume that orders of such a kind were genuine.

The French leaders had spoken similarly only a few weeks before. The French people had not been impressed. The Germans at that time were not just on their doorstep: they were rampaging through the house.

Meanwhile it had been announced that General Sir Edmund Ironside, G.O.C. in C. Home Forces, was organizing for Home Defence small bodies of highly mobile and strongly armed troops, to be called "Ironsides". Many hundreds of these were to be formed from the regular army, and Sir Edmund was sending each "Ironside" a copy of a saying of Oliver Cromwell: "Your danger is as you have seen; and truly I am sorry it is so great. But I wish it to cause no despondency, as truly I think it will not; for we are British . . . it's no longer disputing, but out instantly all you can."

These highly trained, highly mobile troops consisted mainly of soldiers with less than six months' service, poorly equipped, with one or two trucks at their disposal. There were a few hastily built, thinly armoured cars, reminiscent of the "cardboard tanks" used by the Germans on manoeuvres before Hitler came to power, which would not have stopped a sword thrust let alone a rifle bullet. Ironsides? "Old Ironsides" would have been more appropriate.

With France in her death throes, on July 16, 1940, Hitler issued his Directive No. 16. It began:

> As England, in spite of the hopelessness of her military position, has so far shown herself unwilling to come to any compromise, I have decided to begin to prepare for, and if necessary to carry out, an invasion of England.
>
> This operation is dictated by the necessity of eliminating Great Britain as a base from which the war against Germany can be fought, and if necessary the island will be occupied.

Speaking at Lincoln the following day, Sir Nevile Henderson, the former British Ambassador to Germany, warned, "Hitler will attempt to invade England this month or next." Sir Nevile was wearing the shapeless denims of the newly formed Local Defence Volunteers, who were hopefully dubbed "parashots" by the Press. "Hitler cannot win the war," he went on, "unless he can defeat the British, and he can only defeat the British by starving us, by blockade, by bombing us into submission or by coming and invading this country. In my

opinion he is going try all these three moves. If I have any knowledge of Germans and Hitler, the Fuehrer's main and ultimate object is Britain."

The same day the Press asked the War Office if any statement could be made on the Government's plans for the training of men of fighting age. A spokesman told them that the whole matter was under consideration and that he did not know when an official statement could be made.

That night Winston Churchill broadcast a short message to the nation, which was relayed to the United States, "We shall fight on unconquerable," he said.

The following night Churchill rammed home the message with a broadcast which concluded with the words, "Let us brace ourselves to our duty and so bear ourselves that if the British Commonwealth and Empire lasts for a thousand years, men will still say: This was their finest hour."

Meanwhile, even as a thoroughly demoralized and disintegrated France waited anxiously for the Germans to grant their request for an armistice, it was still being reported in the British Press that French troops were tired but holding on everywhere, that half a million French fortress troops had escaped the German trap in Alsace Lorraine, and that General Weygand was planning to "pin" the eastern wing of a new line in the southern Jura mountains.

On June 18, the Ministry of Home Security issued seven basic rules that all civilians must obey if and when German forces landed in this country, with the exhortation that these orders should be carried out both in the spirit and in the letter as they were every bit as important as those given to men of the Armed Forces. Householders were sent a leaflet containing the instructions, which were as follows:

1. If the Germans come by parachute, aeroplane or ship, you must remain where you are. The order is "stay put".

The Commander-in-Chief will tell you if evacuation is necessary.

If you run away you will be exposed to far greater danger, because you will be machine-gunned from the air as were civilians in Holland and Belgium, and you will also block the roads by which our own armies will advance to turn the Germans out.

2. Do not believe rumours, and do not spread them. When you receive an order, make quite sure that it is a true order and not a faked one.

Most of you know your policemen and your A.R.P. wardens by sight. You can trust them. If you keep your heads you can also tell whether a military officer is really British or only pretending to be so. If in doubt, ask the policeman or the A.R.P. warden. Use your common sense.

3. Keep watch. If you see anything suspicious, note it carefully and go at once to the nearest police officer or station, or to the nearest military officer – not your neighbours.

Train yourself to notice the exact time and place where you saw anything suspicious. Be calm, quick and exact.

4. Do not give any German anything. Do not tell him anything. Hide your food and your bicycles. Hide your maps. See that the enemy gets no petrol.

If you have a car or motor-bicycle, put it out of action when not in use. It is not enough to remove the ignition key. You must make the car useless to anyone but yourself.

5. Be ready to help the military in any way. But do not block roads until ordered to do so by the military or Local Defence Volunteers.

6. In factories and shops all managers and workmen should organise some system now by which a sudden attack can be resisted.

Remember always that parachutists and Fifth Column men can succeed only if they can create disorganisation. Make certain that no suspicious strangers enter your premises.

7. Think before you act. But think always of your country first.

More detailed instructions may, when the time comes, be given you by the military and police authorities.

The second evacuation of children from London, which had taken six days, ended with 340,000 still remaining in Greater London.

17

Plans were made for the evacuation of some children to Canada
but then left in abeyance.

At a meeting in the House of Commons on the night of June 18,
1940, one hundred members of parliament expressed strong feelings
that Local Defence Volunteers should be equipped with rifles and
grenades, instead of the useless assortment of laughable weapons
such as pitchforks, cutlasses, and home-made pikes with which they
had armed themselves. But a request for a wide-scale distribution
of arms to civilians such as the Spanish Government had made during
the Spanish Civil War was not approved, on the ground that weapons
should be restricted to ex-servicemen and others who knew how to
handle them. Indeed, the few weapons which were available were
of 1914–18 vintage.

Military M.P.s who had discussed their position with Mr. Anthony
Eden, the War Minister, told him that their offers to instruct recruits
of the L.D.V. had been rebuffed. And they were not the only ones
to have their offers of help spurned. A letter to a newspaper from
a writer in Harrow-on-the-Hill offered congratulations to a Mr. W.G.
of Bloomsbury, who had been accepted by the L.D.V. because he
was able to supply his own revolver. The writer stated that he too
could have supplied his own revolver, but although a registered
holder for many years, he had been asked to hand it over to the
police. He added that he had served in colonial volunteer units
and had competed at Bisley meetings.

A leader in one of the dailies said of the British Army recently
evacuated from the Continent to home ground: "These men know
what fighting is. They know what the Germans are. Their blood is
up. They want a return match to compensate for that in which they
fought so gallantly and with so little luck."

"Play the game, you cads! Be sporting, you Germans. We want a return match on our home ground." Perhaps we were fortunate that the Germans did not oblige.

Announcing the Government's new emergency food scheme, Mr. Robert Boothby, Parliamentary Secretary to the Ministry of Food, stated that although there would be no immediate new rationing all food growers must understand that there was no such phrase as "too much" and that all surplus produce would be collected, sold, and consumed. Not a carrot or an onion would be wasted. That was long-term planning indeed, saving carrots and onions. With the Germans already smashing at the doors and windows of the house, householders were stocking their larders and being told to fight from room to room, up the stairs, on the landings, and if necessary on the roof.

Frantic efforts were made to meet the menace of a German invasion. On May 31, 1940, orders had been given for signposts throughout the country to be taken down, and names of streets, railway stations, and villages obliterated. Not until October 1942 were signs in some rural and urban areas permitted, and only in 1944 were all place-name restrictions lifted. As the Germans did not come the ploy only succeeded in baffling travellers and drivers from different parts of the country.

Trenches were dug and pill-boxes were built facing every direction up hill and down dale, and if the defenders found they were facing the wrong way when the enemy landed, they would just have to sort things out the best way they could. Further preparations were made to cope with air raids. Coffins and mass graves were prepared for the victims of total war.

At the cinema people had seen newsreels of war in China, Abyssinia, Spain, Poland, Norway, Belgium, and France, and so they had some idea of the havoc and horror that might be in store for them; yet somehow the reality of it seemed remote. The storm and stench of battle, tanks rumbling through towns and villages, families torn asunder, and refugees choking the roads and lanes as they streamed desperately to nowhere, was something that happened in other countries. Air raids could be expected – but invasion? Well, perhaps, but it did not seem like something that would really happen. It was not an eventuality that was easy for the British mind to accept. German troops marching down Oxford Street, concentration camps in Hyde Park, the German flag flying over Buckingham Palace, belonged in the works of William Le Queux and H. G. Wells, and in the "bloods".

Some of the ideas for coping with the invincible exponents of the *Blitzkrieg* too might have been conjured up in Cloud-cuckoo-land. Soldiers were actually ordered to hide the bolts of their rifles in order to render them useless to German paratroopers, who, armed with Schmeisser machine-pistols, would have had about as much use for the antiquated British Lee-Enfield as they would for a blunderbuss. Many were the British soldiers who went on parade with a useless rifle, having forgotten to replace the bolt left hidden under a blanket. Sentries were also ordered to remove the slings from their rifles, on the reasoning that they would thus be compelled to carry their rifles ready to hand in case of sudden attack. But unable to carry his rifle slung, a sentry would often just stand his rifle against a wall. A system was devised for carrying a clumsy gas cape at the alert. This was rolled and carried across the top of the haversack worn on the back in battle order, with a string attached by a slip-knot. A quick tug at the string was supposed to send the cape swishing down the soldier's back, whereupon he would slip swiftly into the voluminous sleeves, press the press-studs, and hey presto! he was ready for a mustard gas attack – provided he had put on his respirator, donned his gas gloves, and taken a swift sniff to make sure it was mustard gas not phosgene, D.M., chlorine, or some other unidentifiable toxic gas. Unfortunately the string gimmick never worked. A yank at the string and the cape remained securely knotted at the nape of the soldier's neck. Gas capes were useful only in case of rain, when troops were not really allowed to use them anyway, having instead to rely on smelly rubberized waterproof ground sheets that dangled unevenly from their shoulders, dripped water down their necks, and soaked them practically from waist to boots.

Whatever orders did come down from the big brains higher up regarding matters such as these, the average soldier was practical and capable enough to cope with problems in his own way, and being part of a unit he was quickly able to adapt himself to meeting daily assaults on his intelligence. Civilians, however, were more likely to obey unfamiliar orders and requests to the letter, useless as such orders might be. Gas masks in their tatty cardboard boxes were carried about by civilians, long after soldiers were using their respirator cases as shoulder-bags for carrying civvy shoes, cigarettes, and other sundries to dances. By the time the civilians discarded their useless respirators, many were minus the eyepiece, snoutless, or without their elastic straps.

Blackout regulations were strictly enforced to the point of utter stupidity. Any person lighting a cigarette during a blackout could find himself being dressed down by a nervous but pompous air raid warden, as if the cigarette had been a signal for German aircraft, not even in the vicinity, to hurl down a rain of bombs.

Every civilian carried a National Registration card and was issued with a ration card; soldiers carried their A.B.64s. People often carried the address of their next of kin.

Cars were ordered to be immobilized at night, or if left unattended, by removal of the rotor arm, and prosecutions for failing to do so often resulted in heavy fines. In the event of an emergency such as an enemy landing, cars were to be rendered useless, and it was suggested that one way to do this was to puncture the petrol tank with a nail.

Houses were prepared against bomb blast by sandbagging, criss-crossing the windows with adhesive tape, and buttressing the ceilings with beams. In readiness for fires caused by incendiary bombs, shovels, buckets of sand, and water were placed at strategic points, and attics and lofts were cleared of combustible junk. Although people were warned against hoarding food, many people contrived to keep a small stock of tinned goods and some tea just in case of emergencies. Additional air raid shelters were prepared in streets, gardens, and backyards.

Civilians were ordered to hand over to the police all weapons, including sporting guns, and binoculars and compasses were also called in, as well as fireworks capable of being used for the purpose of giving visible signals to the enemy. Under new defence regulations no one other than designated persons serving the Crown was permitted to fly a kite or a balloon. This did not please the children.

Farmers were instructed by the Government how to proceed in the event of a German invasion. The Ministry of Agriculture issued a notice informing them that unless military action in the immediate neighbourhood made it impossible, they and their farm-hands must go on with their tasks of ploughing, sowing, cultivating, hoeing, and harvesting as in normal times. Most of the countless directives, documents, and pamphlets issued were regarded as useless by the recipients and were ignored, and many people wondered why at such a grave time, when manpower and material were so valuable, so much was wasted churning out useless "bumpf".

It is understandable, in the light of the extraordinary circumstances arising from the confusion after Dunkirk, the collapse of France, and the imminent invasion, that Whitehall should have continued to pile up its record of blunders and mistakes, and the bewildered civilians did their best to comply with even the most piffling of instructions. It was a case of the blind leading the blind. Gradually, however, some semblance of order was created out of chaos, and more realistic preparations were made to meet invaders, but bungling, poor co-ordination, sketchy details, and lack of cohesive plans were still inevitable. Apart from the Army, Navy, and Air Force, the Home Guard, the police, and the civil defence services – local government, factories, railways, and mines all had their roles and duties to be considered in the overall strategy of meeting a serious German invasion.

The question of who did what, where, and when was extremely difficult to resolve, and it was a herculean task to make ready for every contingency that might arise in the event of simultaneous landings by air and sea in various parts of the country. To even conceive how liaison and contacts could be maintained between fighting forces, lines of supply and communications, workers in field and factory, food supplies to maintain a civilian population, the distribution services, with ruptured road and rail links, not to mention streams of refugees, the homeless, and the wounded, seemed impossible.

And the situation would be worse if the country were to be truncated by the enemy with docks and railheads lost or destroyed.

The problems were formidable, yet even as Britain was preparing to meet invaders she was already hard at work making herself into a base from which the reconquest of Europe could be launched. Perhaps at the back of most Britons' minds was the conviction that there could be no successful invasion of Britain: perhaps it was wishful thinking. Certainly there was no panic in advance. But abroad the invasion of Britain was considered inevitable.

On May 17, 1940, the United States Embassy had advised all American citizens in Great Britain that the time had come to return home. They were advised to leave as soon as possible by way of Eire. Those who were unable to leave England were urged to move as far away as they could from metropolitan centres and complexes likely to be considered by the Germans as of military importance, and to seek accommodation in rural areas. On July 7, a grim warning was given to Americans that they might now be facing their last opportunity to get home before the end of the war, and most felt reluctantly compelled to heed the warning. There were many who decided to stick it out, however, although the consensus of American opinion was that the chances of Britain's survival in the impending struggle were not high.

The Americans choosing to stay on in Britain were made of stern stuff. Early in June the first American Squadron of the Home Guard, the Eagle Squadron, with a strength of sixty men, was formed in London under the command of General Wade H. Hayes. The formation of this unit did not please the Foreign Office, who thought that it would be difficult to deny the same right to any other sizeable bodies of foreign nationals, for example the Japanese. Joseph Kennedy, the American Ambassador, also disapproved of the American unit, because he felt that all U.S. citizens might be shot as *francs-tireurs* when the Germans occupied London. He saw the occupation as inevitable.

Nevertheless, as the storm gathered, it seemed to the rest of the world that Britons simply did not grasp the fact that Britain faced impending doom. They went about their daily tasks, apparently serene and confident that, relieved of useless Continental allies, they had been left unhampered to face the Hun in single combat. In fact, however, Britain did not stand alone after the collapse of France: Imperial troops were already in Britain, and more were on their way, bringing new heart to the beleaguered island. The Empire was behind Britain, not one member suggesting that she should yield to Germany. Imperial troops poured into the Middle East, supplying necessary reinforcements and shouldering responsibilities that lightened the burdens of Britain. Forces from Canada and Australia, South Africa and Rhodesia, India, and dozens of smaller countries were ranged against Britain's enemies.

But the threats facing Britain were daunting: invasion and all it

Memories of pictures like this one of British Fascists at a Nazi rally in Nuremberg in 1934 contributed to British fears of a fifth column.

brought with it – mass bombing, inexorable tanks, chemical and bacteriological warfare, death and destruction, concentration camps, mass executions, and treachery from within. The only alternative to battle was surrender to the Nazis, and only a few, mostly Fascists, were prepared to do that.

Although Britons seemed to be facing their future with some equanimity, there was a desperate fear they hardly dared contemplate, and that was for the fate of their children. They felt that if only the children could be evacuated to a place of safety away from the bombs, tanks, and vengeful Germans, the decks could be cleared for action and they could fight on with clear resolve. Machinery was set up to carry out such an evacuation, and the Dominions and Canada were ready to play their parts. But when 200,000 applications were made by parents to the Children's Overseas Reception Board,

23

the Government expressed surprise at the large number of applicants. It was announced early in July that no more applications could be accepted for the time being. Yet 200,000 children represented only a small proportion of those children eligible for evacuation, so why the Government should have been surprised by the number of applicants is not clear. As it happened, by the time the scheme was brought into operation people's confidence that they could weather the storm had returned, and second thoughts about sending children across the Atlantic, through U-boat-infested waters, turned the proposed mass evacuation into a trickle. Fewer than 8,000 children, between the ages of five and fifteen, finally sailed for the Dominions, Canada, and the United States.

The Germans refused an American request to give the boats carrying evacuees a safe conduct, realistically stating that to do so would be to relieve Britain of an enormous worry and to strengthen her power to resist Germany. The tragedy which so many people had feared struck when, after all 390 children were rescued from one torpedoed ship another, the *City of Benares*, was sunk by a U-boat on September 17, 1940, with a loss of 260 lives. Only eleven of the eighty-four children on board were rescued. On October 2, all further Government-sponsored evacuation was stopped, and the American voluntary organizations which had helped in the evacuations suspended their activities a week later. Some wealthier families were still able to send their children abroad by private arrangement.

Children had been moved out of London and other big cities and people had been evacuated from the South and East coasts at the start of the war, but many had moved back during the period of the "phoney war", which lasted until April 1940. With the threat of invasion, once more children had been evacuated from London to homes in the West Country, yet during July and August 1940 when the Battle of Britain was being fought and towns were being hit in daylight raids, the rate of evacuation slowed down. Later, as Londoners became used to air raids and to sheltering in the Underground, they were loath to send their reluctant children to live in an unfamiliar and often unfriendly atmosphere, preferring them to remain in familiar surroundings so that families could take their chances together. Most parents, having once experienced the disruption and sorrow of parting with their children, did not wish to part with them again.

But if the people could not be saved from the Germans, money could. A preparation for invasion which the Government deemed necessary was to send all the gold held in the banks to Canada. Also consigned to vaults in Montreal were the nation's entire holdings of foreign securities. The first shipment was made in the cruiser *Emerald* on June 24, followed by further consignments in warships and merchantmen. Not a ship was lost, and the vast treasure, estimated to value seven billion pounds, was moved to safety.

Many of the well-heeled were able to find cosy retreats in country

The Battle of Britain—a re-enactment from the film of that title.

hotels, houses, and cottages, and were not very happy when evacuees from working-class areas of the cities, or common soldiers, were billeted in their vicinity. Perhaps they considered that scrounging eggs, butter, and poultry from neighbouring farms was their prerogative and that Cockney kids and soldiers lowered the tone of the neighbourhood, anyway.

In June 1940 the ringing of church bells was banned and was henceforth to be used only by the military and the police as a warning of enemy attacks by air or sea. Soon everyone was straining his ears thinking he could hear the sound of bells in the distance, and, in fact, on September 7, 1940, bells were rung to the consternation

The British fleet showing its teeth on the eve of war.

of many people who thought "*Der Tag*" had finally arrived. It was a false alarm. A few days later the wild bells rang out again; another false alarm. The use of church bells as an invasion warning system was dropped on April 4, 1943, and churches reclaimed their bells to call the faithful.

There were those to whom it was unthinkable that in time of crisis and imminent invasion sporting events should be allowed to continue. Letters to the Press deplored the fact that there was still horse racing, greyhound racing, and cricket, that wasters and idlers were being allowed to attend sporting gatherings. But the other side of the coin was spun to show that most of the so-called idlers and wasters were war workers and servicemen on leave enjoying a little well-earned relaxation. On June 19, 1940, a stop was put to horse racing, though other forms of sport and entertainment were allowed to continue. As far as the exigencies of the services allowed, servicemen indulged in all their usual sporting activities, and even played football as well as cricket, throughout the hot, critical summer of 1940.

Soon after the outbreak of war all poisonous reptiles, deadly spiders, scorpions, rats, and other rodent pests had been destroyed at the London Zoo. In the event of bombing nobody wanted the additional menace of the deadly breeds creeping and crawling out over the city to propagate and proliferate. When the air raids

26

did begin in earnest, the big cats, bears, apes, and other dangerous beasts were locked in their inner dens at night to make escape more difficult should the Zoo be hit by bombs. The Zoo maintained on its staff a few trained marksmen to deal with dangerous escapees, perhaps crazed by the bombing. During raids the Zoo was hit a number of times, but casualties were light. A few birds escaped from their cages; a zebra bolted when the Zebra House was hit, but was recaptured without much trouble; and when Monkey Hill received a direct hit the monkeys, quite unperturbed, just went about their monkey business as usual.

With the start of heavy air raids on London, most theatres, cinemas, and other places of entertainment felt obliged to close their doors, but before long, as people began to recover from their initial shock, like the monkeys at the Zoo, it was business as usual again. Some theatres opened for performances during the day, and the first of the midday concerts were given at the National Gallery, as well as a midday ballet at the Arts Theatre Club, which was all very pleasing to a tiny minority. At the Windmill Theatre in the West End of London the show went on as usual, providing nudity and crudity for a slightly larger minority. This theatre boasted that throughout the war it never closed. Perhaps an O.B.E. should have been forthcoming for someone or other on that score.

Naturally, at this time there was a good deal of extra confusion and bumbling. Some officials, both military and civil, seemed to be running in circles or hither and thither issuing orders and counter-orders in a non-system of trial and error. However, valuable work was done and valuable experience was gained, and if there was confusion there was little sign of panic as the assault against Britain increased in intensity.

Of course, everyone was made acutely aware that the enemy could descend from the skies at any time; that enemy agents would be roaming the countryside dressed as nuns, as the Press had reported they were doing in the Low Countries during the *Blitzkrieg*; that fifth-columnists were lurking on street corners ready to "do the dirty".

Flares over aerodromes were reported as descending enemy parachutists. Spies were seen hiding behind bushes, lapping up beer and information in pubs, and flashing signals at night to enemy aircraft. At Bucklands, near Dover, a mysterious light was reported to have been seen on the outskirts of the town. Soldiers sent to investigate discovered that the light had been from a candle held by an old man going out back to the privy. He was highly indignant when warned not to use a candle in the future, and when he complained that once in the dark he had fallen over a bucket and sprained his ankle an irreverent soldier told him to stay indoors and use a "po".

A motorist who failed to stop when a sentry waved him down one wet and windy night at a road block near Swingate Inn on the Dover road had a bullet put through a rear mudguard of his car. It turned out that the shaken motorist was employed at the harbour and was

DANGER of INVASION

Last year all who could be spared from this town were asked to leave, not only for their own safety, but so as to ease the work of the Armed Forces in repelling an invasion.

The danger of invasion has increased and the Government requests all who can be spared, and have somewhere to go. to leave without delay.

This applies particularly to :—
SCHOOL CHILDREN
MOTHERS WITH YOUNG CHILDREN
AGED AND INFIRM PERSONS
PERSONS LIVING ON PENSIONS
PERSONS WITHOUT OCCUPATION
          OR IN RETIREMENT

If you are one of these, you should arrange to go to some other part of the country. You should not go to the coastal area of East Anglia, Kent or Sussex.

School children can be registered to join school parties in the reception areas, and billets will be found for them.

If you are in need of help you can have your railway fare paid and a billeting allowance paid to any relative or friend with whom you stay.

If you are going, go quickly.

Take your
NATIONAL REGISTRATION IDENTITY CARD
RATION BOOK
GAS MASK

ALSO any bank book, pension payment order book, insurance cards, unemployment book, military registration documents, passport, insurance policies, securities and any ready money.

If your house will be left unoccupied, turn off gas, electricity and water supplies and make provision for animals and birds. Lock your house securely. Blinds should be left up, and if there is a telephone line, ask the telephone exchange to disconnect it.

Apply at the Local Council Offices for further information.

Private Car and Motor Cycle owners who have not licensed their vehicles and have no petrol coupons may be allowed to use their cars unlicensed for one journey only and may apply to the Police for petrol coupons to enable them to secure sufficient petrol to journey to their destination.

ESSENTIAL WORKERS MUST STAY
particularly the following classes :—
Members of the Home Guard
Observer Corps
Coastguards, Coast Watchers and Lifeboat Crews
Police and Special Constabulary
Fire Brigade and Auxiliary Fire Service
A.R.P. and Casualty Services
Members of Local Authorities and their officials and employees
Workers on the land
Persons engaged on war work, and other essential services
Persons employed by contractors on defence work
Employees of water, sewerage, gas & electricity undertakings
Persons engaged in the supply and distribution of food
Workers on export trades
Doctors, Nurses and Chemists
Ministers of Religion
Government Employees
Employees of banks
Employees of transport undertakings,
    namely railways, docks, canals, ferries,
    and road transport (both passenger and goods).

When invasion is upon us it may be necessary to evacuate the remaining population of this and certain other towns. Evacuation would then be compulsory at short notice, in crowded trains, with scanty luggage, to destinations chosen by the Government. If you are not among the essential workers mentioned above, it is better to go now while the going is good.

AUCKLAND GEDDES,
REGIONAL COMMISSIONER FOR CIVIL DEFENCE,
TUNBRIDGE WELLS,
MARCH, 1941.

Hedy Lamarr.

Rita Hayworth.

on his way to work on the night shift. The officer in charge of the post gave the sentry a "rocket" and told him to "boil out" his rifle and report to him with it clean first thing in the morning.

Rumours abounded of spies being arrested as they landed by boat or dropped by parachute and of spies caught prowling around military establishments and installations. As there were service establishments practically everywhere, any harmless civilian pausing to tie a shoelace could find himself under suspicion. Near Nettlebed, Oxfordshire, on July 1, 1940, a young man was arrested as a "spy", and he implicated a local farmer. It transpired that the "spy", a parson's son, was an Army deserter on the run and no more a spy than the irate farmer he had implicated, whose ruffled dignity was only restored by the award of a goodly sum as damages by the Army Council. The young man was courtmartialled for his trouble and sent to prison for two years.

When a Junkers 88 was forced down at Graveney Marsh in Kent, the German crew, intent on destroying their aircraft before it could fall into British hands, opened fire on men of the Royal Ulster Rifles as they approached the machine. In the short exchange of small-arms fire that followed, two of the Germans were wounded. The plane was recovered intact after a British officer had dismantled the two time bombs in it which the Germans had been trying to activate.

Soldiers and civilians were warned not to pick up fountain pens, pencils, and other small objects such as cigarette lighters, boxes of matches, and packets of cigarettes as it was possible they were booby traps dropped by the enemy. At first when the enemy flew sorties over the South-East Coast, soldiers blazed away with rifles and bren-guns at low-flying German aircraft which often strafed parade grounds, vehicles, and working parties of soldiers. A favourite target of yellow-nosed Messerschmitts were the barrage balloons over Dover and Folkestone. One day a furious Canadian fighter pilot who had just baled out of his aircraft stormed into a military camp near Dover and demanded to know who was the "silly sod" who had shot him down from inside the camp. A corporal on a bren had already claimed the Canadian's Hurricane as a Messerschmitt. From the same camp, another bren had accounted for a barrage balloon flown from the camp. The bren-gunner, who had been hopefully firing at a Messerschmitt, did not claim the balloon as a Zeppelin. Soldiers soon stopped trying to pot enemy aircraft with rifles, not so much because it was a useless exercise as because it meant "boiling out" their weapons afterwards to stop the barrels from sweating; a tedious task.

Early in September a new crop of rumours began to spread inland from the South Coast. The latest "griff", as the Army called it, or the latest "gen", as the R.A.F. called it, was that the bodies of large numbers of German soldiers had been washed up on the beaches or had been recovered floating in the harbours along the South Coast. It was reported that most of the bodies were burned and charred as a result of the R.A.F.'s setting the sea ablaze and engulfing German invasion barges trying to cross the Channel. As it was not uncommon for dead airmen to be washed ashore, it is not impossible that a few corpses swelled into hundreds, increasing at each telling. At Dover there was a rumour that Germans, in a commando-type raid, had landed at Rye – or was it Deal? (or was it St. Margaret's Bay or Folkestone?) – and had snatched British soldiers and taken them back to France as prisoners.

There were also rumours that fifth-columnists who had advanced plans to receive the German invaders had been on the alert, but had had to scurry back into their holes when the "invasion" failed. All the same, it was said, the traitors were busy preparing additional "black lists" to supplement those already in the hands of the German security forces, and they were feeding fat morsels of useful information to German spies.

There were real spies as well as rumoured ones, however, coming across from the Continent and Norway in submarines and fishing boats and landing by dinghy on isolated beaches. Two spies landed near Hythe in September 1940, and within hours were taken prisoner by a patrol of the Somerset Light Infantry. Two more spies came ashore near Dungeness on the same day. One was captured the next morning as he was trying to get a drink after hours at a public house in Lydd, and the other was caught the following day. All four spies were tried and three of them were sentenced to death and executed. On the night of September 30, two men and a woman who had been flown by seaplane from Norway were put ashore by rubber dinghy on the coast of Banffshire. A few hours later they were in custody.

But, of course, not all spies were caught, and not all fifth-columnists and potential traitors were interned. The Germans received intelligence from their agents in Britain, some of it valuable, and other information was supplied by Nazi sympathizers.

One serious instance of espionage concerned Tyler Kent, an American cypher clerk employed in the U.S. Embassy in London; Anna Wolkoff, the daughter of a former Russian Admiral; and a member of parliament, Captain Ramsey. They were members of the "Right Club", a clique of rabid anti-Semites. Wolkoff was in contact with the Italian Embassy in Rome, and with William Joyce, the British traitor known as Lord Haw-Haw, who broadcast German propaganda to Britain from Hamburg. Kent, who kept copies of secret documents transmitted to and from America, professed to have been motivated by his disapproval of American policies. Wolkoff was an ardent pro-German and anti-Jew. Captain Ramsey, an old Etonian and ex–World War I officer who was the M.P. for Peebles and Midlothian, was a virulent anti-Semite who let his hatred of the Jews override his patriotism although he was no Nazi sympathizer. He was chiefly interested in the Right Club as an anti-Semitic action group whose main purpose seemed to be crawling out nightly into the blackout

What do
I do...

if I hear news
that Germans are
trying to land,
or have landed?

I remember that this is the moment to act like a soldier. I do *not* get panicky. I *stay put*. I say to myself: Our chaps will deal with them. I do *not* say: "I must get out of here." I remember that fighting men must have clear roads. I do *not* go on to the road on bicycle, in car or on foot. Whether I am at work or at home, I just *stay put*.

Cut this out—and keep it!

Issued by The Ministry of Information.
Space presented to the Nation by The Brewers' Society.

to flypost walls with bills proclaiming that the war was a "Jews' War" and to scrawl Fascist slogans on lavatory walls.

Kent and Wolkoff were arrested on May 18, 1940. Kent's diplomatic immunity was waived by the American Ambassador and he was sentenced to seven years' imprisonment. Wolkoff was sentenced to three. It could not be proved that Captain Ramsey had broken any laws; he was interned on May 23 and not released until after the war.

As first Norway and then France fell to the Germans, a huge round-up was ordered throughout Britain of everybody who could be classed as an alien. The field was wide. Included in the host of people taken into custody were Italians who had lived in Britain for years, Jewish refugees from Germany, and other victims of Nazi persecution, as well as anti-Nazis from Austria, Czechoslovakia, and Hungary. Families were broken up, individuals useful to the British war effort were snatched from their work, and injustices and indignities were inflicted on a bewildered group of people who were obviously no threat to British security. Petty tyrants, unsympathetic bureaucrats, and "rubber stamps" had a field day as luckless aliens were harassed, bullied, and humiliated. Officialdom thought it necessary, in the light of fifth-columnist activities in the *Blitzkrieg*, not to risk the possibility of even one potential fifth-columnist remaining at large. But it was the manner in which the operation was carried out and the behaviour of some spiteful xenophobes that upset a large number of the British public and a vast number of people friendly to Britain abroad.

Some eight thousand aliens, many innocent of hostility to British war aims, were shipped to Canada and Australia. A number, including innocent victims of the indiscriminate round-up, lost their lives when the *Arandora Star*, a former cruise liner, was torpedoed by an Italian submarine in July 1940.

Churchill himself said that he knew that a great many people who had been detained were passionate enemies of Nazi Germany. He was sorry for them, but he could not at that time and under the existing stress draw all the distinctions he would like to see made. If parachute landings were attempted and fierce fighting followed, he went on, those unfortunate people would be far better out of the way for their own sakes as well as for the sake of the British people. There was another class for which he did not feel the slightest sympathy, he added: Parliament had granted powers to put down fifth-column activities with a strong hand, and these powers would be used without hesitation until there was complete satisfaction that the malignancy had been effectively stamped out. Harsh times meant no time for finesse. Especially in total war did the innocent have to suffer with the guilty.

The radio played a big part in the war. Everyone listened religiously to the frequent news broadcasts, which actually told little but made the public feel it was being informed up to the minute. With the prospect of invasion following the Continental debacle, every newscaster announced his name before reading the news bulletins. This was a precaution in case the enemy or fifth-columnists seized Broadcasting House and broadcast false information or instructions and misleading statements to an unsuspecting public. People soon came to recognize the voices of Alvar Lidell, Frank Phillips, Bruce Belfrage, and Stuart Hibberd and would listen to programmes just to hear the voices of their favourite announcers.

Arandora Star
THE WORLD'S MOST DELIGHTFUL CRUISING LINER

PROGRAMME OF
SUNSHINE CRUISES

Perfect cuisine and service, luxurious appointments, endless entertainments

OCTOBER 12
30 DAYS from 55 GNS.

Barcelona, Naples, Alexandria, Jaffa (for Jerusalem), Cyprus, Port Said, Haifa (for Nazareth), Beyrout, Rhodes, Athens, Malta, Algiers, Lisbon (for Estoril).

DECEMBER 20
Annual Xmas Cruise
20 DAYS from 34 GNS.

Madeira, Gambia (Bathurst), Sierra Leone (Freetown), Teneriffe, Santa Cruz de la Palma.

Special Winter Holiday Cruise to
HONOLULU

LEAVING SOUTHAMPTON JAN. 22. 75 DAYS from 153 GUINEAS.

To MADEIRA, MIAMI (for PALM BEACH, Florida), HAVANA, PANAMA, SAN FRANCISCO, LOS ANGELES (for Hollywood and Pasadena), MAZATLAN (for Mexico City), MANZANILLA, ACAPULCO, SAN JOSE (for Guatemala), LA LIBERTAD (for San Salvador), CURACAO, TENERIFFE.

BLUE STAR LINE

3, Lower Regent Street, London, S.W.1.   Whitehall 2266.   Liverpool, Birmingham, Manchester, Glasgow, Bradford, Belfast, Paris and all Travel Agencies.

C.F.H. 50

Pre-war advertisement for a holiday cruise on the ill-fated *Arandora Star*.

After Dunkirk, Britain was wide open to a German invasion. The army which had been evacuated from the Continent was a well-defeated army which had lost most of its equipment and weapons and was even less capable of withstanding the victorious Germans than it had been in France and Belgium. Conscripts had not finished their training and were barely equipped with uniforms let alone the minimum requirement of a rifle and a few bandoliers of ammunition. The R.A.F. were in no position to defend their aerodromes against advancing German tanks, and in the Battle of Britain had scarcely enough planes to defend the skies over Britain even without having to split their forces to counter a seaborne attack. The Navy, coping desperately with U-boats and raiders, would have faced problems in the Channel such as the *Repulse* and the *Renown* had to face off Malaya later in the war.

When the threat to Britain was greatest, instructions to the public were often vague, equivocal, and confusing, and sometimes downright contradictory.

On July 11, *The Times* carried this official advertisement to the public:

What do I do?
I remember that this is the moment to act like a soldier. I do *not* get panicky. I *stay put*. I do *not* say: "I must get out of here".
I remember that fighting men must have clear roads. I do *not* go on to the road on a bicycle, in a car, or on foot, whether I am *at* work or at home I just *stay put*.

Stay put for what? To be left in German hands? To be caught in a crossfire between opposing forces? To be pinned down in a battle zone?

A few days after the advertisement had appeared, Churchill had something to say on the subject. In his broadcast of July 14, 1940, he said that we should defend every street, every town, and every village. Other leaders were exhorting the public to participate whole-heartedly in slaughtering German invaders by any means.

Yet for all the fine words there was really very little the public could have done that would have been effective against the ruthlessness and brutal determination of the German invaders. Fortunately for this country, although Britons' courage and fortitude were tested time and time again, the grim experience of trying to stop the Nazi march through their own embattled homeland was one they did not have to face.

Keep the
Home Guards burning

IN 1941 OUR UNIT WAS ENGAGED IN A SERIES OF TRAINING exercises consisting mainly of stunts such as scaling a cliff overhung with rolls of barbed wire to raid an airfield above, landing by dinghy to put a coastal battery out of action by planting "time bombs" where it would hurt most then stealing off into the night, and other amusing capers dreamed up in the devious but fertile brain of our energetic officer in charge. Then one day it was decided by the powers upstairs that while we were going about playing our little games it would be a good idea to test the Home Guard in the area.

So one dark night we found ourselves on the roof of a building used by the Home Guard as a store, forcing open a skylight. As I weighed the least in our happy little band, I was elected "Joe Soap", a rope was lowered into the darkness of the room below, and I climbed down it. It was a bruising experience as there was too much rope above and not enough below and I fell the last few feet.

"Sh! Not so much row!" called our officer.

I answered with a single word which was, however, in the plural, and switched on my torch.

"Psst!" went our officer. "Turn that light off."

I groped around in the gloom. The place was cluttered up, and I kept falling over objects which seemed to have been placed to make an obstacle course.

"What's up down there?" called the officer impatiently.

The men giggled.

"Shut your noise!" he hissed, and to me he called, "What can you see, Anglo?"

"Not much unless I switch on the torch, sir," I replied.

"Every unit has a clown," said our officer, "and you're not it. Get on with it."

I switched on the torch and shone it here and there. The room was an Aladdin's cave of Army junk.

"Well," called the officer in a hoarse stage whisper, "what's down there, for chrissake?"

"Cases of ammo, grenades, hurricane lamps, blankets, webbing, clothing, and other odds and sods," I whispered back.

"Up with the ammo and grenades," called our leader.

"Let down more rope," I said.

Soon the ammo and grenades were hauled up to the roof. It was a noisy and precarious business.

"That the lot?" called the officer.

"Well," I said, "there are some good greatcoats and –"

"Don't need any," said the officer. "Up with you!"

"I need a coat, sir," I pleaded. "I need a coat badly. Mine's tatty, tight under the arms, and it's like a tent round the bottom. It looks like it's been slept in for a year, which it has –"

"No coat," came the reply; "that would be stealing."

"Nossir," I said. "A soldier's coat is Army property and is a soldier, for the use of. Any soldier. I'm a soldier and I need a coat."

While I had been talking I had hurriedly tried on a few and had found one which seemed satisfactory.

"All right," grumbled our leader. "Grab a coat, and while you're about it see if there are any battledress blouses about. Chest forty to forty-two. They're always handy."

All we had to remove our booty with was a trek-cart we had borrowed from a builder's yard. It made an awful racket as we hauled it through the deserted streets, but we got back to the hotel where we were billeted without being challenged except by one of our own sentries in the car park.

"Halt! –" he started to yell.

"Shut your noise, Elliot," snapped our leader. "Do you want to wake up the whole town?"

We unloaded the cart and dumped our booty in a shed.

"Right," said our energetic officer, "now for our next port of call."

"Sir!" we protested.

"Get rolling," he grinned.

So off we went again, with the noise of the rattling cart echoing through the empty streets. Our faces (blackened to make ourselves "less conspicuous", we were told) poured perspiration. Not a soul was about. It was eerie. We came down to the sea wall, where there was a large concrete blockhouse with boarded apertures and a pad-locked door. It took a couple of minutes to unscrew the hinges on the door, and before long once more our trusty trek-cart was loaded with boxes of ammunition, grenades, and also a Vickers machine-gun of 1914–18 vintage.

"That's another Home Guard establishment disestablished," said our officer with satisfaction, adding, "Jolly good training, this." And back towards our billets we trundled. About half-way back the cart keeled over as a wheel came off, and the load tipped into the road with a crash. We rushed off into the shadows to take up firing positions. Nothing stirred, so after a while we came back to the wreckage of the cart. It was obviously no use to us any more.

"Right!" snapped our intrepid officer. "Nothing else for it but to hump the lot back to billets, so start humping. It's not all that far. One of you stay and get the cart and the rest of the stuff to the side of the road and keep guard until we get back."

I stayed. I had slipped on my new overcoat to make sure nobody else nicked it, and I was feeling warm and uncomfortable although the only equipment I was carrying was a Tommy gun. As soon as the rest of the boys had disappeared up the road, with our officer, Desperate Dan, loping along in the lead, I sat on the curb and lit a cigarette. A dog sidled up, curious, and sniffed at me a couple of times. I shooed him off. He went a few yards up the road to a safe distance and bravely started to bark at me. I ignored him. I thought, "I'm glad this isn't for real. If it were, it would not be a new coat I needed but a new pair of trousers."

Back in billets the officer rallied us around him. "Right," he said, "you've done a good job and tomorrow you should get your reward. Parade here in the morning at 0700 hours."

We groaned.

"Shut your noise and wait for it!" said Desperate Dan. "We're going to be hanging around that blockhouse nice and early. There'll be a lot of people about. The big brass are coming down to inspect the local Home Guard and make them feel important."

"The big brass or the Home Guard?" asked a fusilier.

"Both," said the officer. "They'll be zeroing in on that blockhouse, and we'll be there to see the fun."

The next morning we stood unobtrusively with some soldiers from other units and a few civilians as a detachment of the Home Guard paraded on the sea wall near the blockhouse. Soon, striding along the road, came the big brass, trailing a band of local notables which, I believe, included the mayor. (I seem to recall glimpsing a chain of office.)

The Home Guard was duly inspected. We saw a Home Guard officer speak to his sergeant-major, who clicked his heels, saluted, and went marching smartly as any regular up to the blockhouse. The big brass and the retinue were trailing not far behind him. We waited expectantly as the sergeant-major unlocked the padlock, swung open the door, and ducked into the blockhouse. A few seconds later he was back in the street, his face a picture of bewilderment, sorrow, and anger that gave our little lot a great deal of satisfaction as we stood innocently on the sidelines. Hurried consultations: hot words: white-faced whisperings: N.C.O.s dashing off north, south, east, and west. The Home Guard had been caught with its trousers down and had lost all its goodies without a shot being fired.

We nipped off, fast. There was no sense in hanging about gloating for too long. We knew we were going to be blamed, but we did not have to worry — we were fireproof. Desperate Dan filled us in with the details later and concluded: "I can tell you we're not popular with the Home Guard right now, so get this. We've been ordered to do an exercise with them this weekend, and they know all about it.

The threat: German parachute troops in 1940.

They'll be manning road blocks and strong points. Our job is to force a way past them, and I think 'force' is going to be the operative word. Don't underestimate them. A lot of them are youngsters in reserved occupations, whatever that is, and others waiting for their call-up. They're very upset and want their revenge, so watch it. No rifle butts, mind you, but I suggest pickaxe handles might be pretty useful. A crack on the shins can be more effective than a knock on the helmet."

The exercise turned out to be a great success as far as we were concerned. We were told that we put eight Home Guards in hospital. That was really adding injury to insult, "But," said Desperate Dan, "it was all good clean fun and, after all, nobody was killed."

"I feel a bit sorry for them," I said. "I mean, they are on our side, I believe, and – "

"You shut your noise," our officer interrupted. "You," he went on accusingly, "nicked one of their overcoats in cold blood, so don't you start going all religious. When the C.O. notified the Home Guard that we had all their gear and they came to collect it, I don't think they believed me when I had to explain we had not been responsible for the loss of the greatcoat."

"Nor the battledress blouses, sir?" I said.

"Nor the battledress blouses," said Desperate Dan coldly. "Fall out, fusilier."

In May 1940, as the military situation grew daily more hopeless for the Allies, the real danger of enemy parachutists dropping over Britain, and the need for rounding up enemy airmen baling out of stricken aircraft, had to be considered. The enthusiasm of hundreds of men who had written to newspapers suggesting they be enrolled and armed to combat such an eventuality was an opportunity for the Government to channel their resolve into deeds. In 1939 Churchill had suggested the formation of a Home Guard, and on May 14, 1940, Anthony Eden announced on the radio that large numbers of British subjects between the ages of fifteen and sixty-five were invited to come forward and enrol in a new force to be called Local Defence Volunteers.

The day after the broadcast police stations were mobbed by eager men volunteering for service with the L.D.V. The Press immediately dubbed the new force with the swashbuckling name "parashots", though this was a hopeful misnomer as there were few arms for the new recruits. This was fortunate at the time, as British airmen baling out over Britain were just as likely to be targets for the new enthusiasts as the enemy.

Volunteers for the new force included retired officers from World War I who turned up at the recruiting centres resplendent in their old medal-ribbon-bedecked uniforms; men in reserved occupations; men too young for regular military service but eager to take some active part in the war; and older men, many of them ex-servicemen who felt the time had come to "fall in" again. What the L.D.V. lacked in arms they made up for in zeal and optimism, and they began drilling armed with broomsticks, to the amusement of little boys who often tried to join in the fun.

Although the task of organizing the L.D.V. was given to a major-general at the War Office, the rapid pace of its growth was such that units were formed all over the country under the aegis of local military units. These found it expedient to appoint as officers local ex-service officers; business men; farmers of substance; and local publicans who had a large clientele, so that they could gain more recruits and could use the local pub as a very pleasant and useful headquarters. These arbitrarily appointed officers selected their own company and platoon commanders, who in turn appointed N.C.O.s. At the time there was some doubt that the L.D.V. qualified as an irregular force as defined under the Geneva Convention. The Germans had no doubt about that at all. They denounced all units of the new force as "murder bands" of *francs-tireurs* who, when caught, would be shot out of hand.

Being an officer in the L.D.V. could be an expensive business. Officers had to pay their own expenses as little money was forthcoming from the authorities, and this was sufficient to rule out would-be officers of the working class even if they had been invited to accept field rank. In any case, as usual the old school tie counted more than ability. Part-time soldiering was difficult for many men of the L.D.V., some having to work hard at their jobs during the day and drill and perform military duties at night and weekends. For others the L.D.V. was like a jolly club with beer at the local and rambles

A call for better weapons for the L.D.V. reported in the *Daily Sketch* of June 19, 1940.

'GIVE L.D.V. MORE WEAPONS'

VERY strong feeling that the Local Defence Volunteers should be "properly organised" was expressed at a meeting of about 100 M.P.s in the House of Commons last night. The volunteers, it was held, should be equipped with rifles and grenades.

A suggestion for wide distribution of arms to civilians was not approved (writes the DAILY SKETCH political correspondent) on the ground that weapons should be restricted to ex-Servicemen and others who know how to handle them.

'Met With Rebuff'

A committee was set up to draft recommendations which will be put to an adjourned meeting today and then submitted to the Government, probably at the secret session.

Military M.P.s who had discussed their position with Mr. Eden, the War Minister, have told him of their disappointment that when offeing their services to instruct recruits or organise L.D.V. they met with rebuff.

"I want to see plenty of skilled shots so that we can be ready for the Germans when they come," said Mr. T. H. Adamson, head of a Putney firm of builders, last night when the Putney Rifle Club was formed with an initial membership of 42.

Mr. Adamson has formed a rifle club for his own employees.

in the country almost as good as hunting, shooting, and fishing – and there was some of that to be had, too.

Discipline was loose at first. Old soldiers did not take kindly to broomstick drill or to being given orders by portly business men who had no service experience. The new recruits also found their duties piffling and irksome compared with their memories of service in the trenches in World War I. All the same some units benefited by being composed of homogeneous elements. For example, Southern Railways organized its own L.D.V., and the members were put on guard at nearly five hundred strategic or vulnerable points along its miles of tracks. Units composed of farmers, farm workers, gamekeepers, and even poachers, patrolled fields, woods, and country lanes with which they were familiar. Factories were guarded by L.D.V. units formed from management and staff, and mines were the responsibility of units of miners.

The volunteers wore pale khaki brassards marked L.D.V. on shapeless mud-coloured denim suits if they were lucky enough to be issued with them, or on their ordinary civilian jackets if not. Some units were luckier than others with their armament, too. Country units were often able to arm themselves with a variety of shotguns and sporting rifles while other units had to rely on a mixed bag of weapons donated by a willing but not always practical public. Batons, pickaxe handles, knives, and iron bars were commonplace, and many strange weapons – relics of bygone wars – were unearthed. Zulu knobkerries and assegais, Gurkha kukris, vicious coshes used in trench raids in World War I, and ceremonial swords were put at the disposal of the L.D.V. Even bows and arrows were not to be sneezed at. Some units composed of engineering workers improvised their own lethal weapons such as catapults, Molotov cocktails, projectors, and mortars, and even a serviceable anti-tank gun.

The Germans were not unaware of this vast array of L.D.V. weapons ready to meet their invasion, and it was a subject for enemy press and radio humour. The famous German magazine *Signal* published pictures and sarcastic commentaries about the L.D.V. effort and antics.

Armed with their curious weapons the early L.D.V.s prowled the countryside on the lookout for suspicious-looking characters who might be spies or fifth-columnists, to the discomfort of many a luckless tramp. They created barricades which would not have stopped a bicycle, let alone a German tank, and were empowered to set up road blocks and to demand that motorists and cyclists show their identity cards. Anybody failing to halt immediately when challenged by an L.D.V. who chanced to be armed with a rifle was likely to find himself shot at.

Lacking the solid identity and confidence of servicemen, the L.D.V.s were inclined to be bristly and officious, and there were inevitable clashes with servicemen and civilians. They were constantly on the alert for paratroops, fifth-columnists, spies, and careless talkers. Anything falling from or appearing in the sky, such as weather

Churchill inspects his
Home Guard and its version
of a road block.

balloons, puffs of anti-aircraft smoke, and flares, was viewed with some trepidation and suspicion. Every person wandering abroad and every stranger in a pub was suspect, and God help him if he was put to the test and could not pronounce "soothe", "wrong", "wretch", and "rats". As far as the Home Guard was concerned civilian cars had no business on the road.

As the Battle of Britain progressed, more and more Home Guards were issued with rifles. Well pleased to find themselves thus equipped, some were inclined to be trigger happy, and British airmen descending by parachute were in peril. A badly burned young fighter pilot baling out over Hampshire after a dogfight found himself a "sitting duck" for the Home Guard and was lucky to escape with his life. In Kent an airman who descended by parachute came under fire from the Home Guard and had to rush for cover in a ditch. On September 4, 1940, the Air Ministry felt obliged to issue a notice reminding the public that not all parachutists were enemies.

Some Home Guard units recruited and equipped by large industrial and commercial firms were almost like private armies and resented interference by military authorities. Some retired officers continued to wear the uniform and insignia of their old rank while serving as privates in the Home Guard, and they hopefully paraded the streets fishing for salutes from raw servicemen. Some old soldiers long past service suitability found companionship in the Home Guard and refuge from the growing austerity of "civvy street", and with all the willingness in the world would have proved something of a liability in the event of a German invasion – but perhaps no more

41

Home Guard (in steel helmets) and Army (in side hats) pause for a picture during battle training.

so than various so-called specialist Home Guard units, such as the "Red Indian Fighters" and the "Dartmoor Cavalry", scattered up and down the country.

Unquestionably, however, countless Home Guard units did valuable service from the dark days following Dunkirk right up to the time they were disbanded, in December 1944. They released troops from routine guard duties, home defence responsibilities, and sundry other mundane duties, to take part in more extensive training and preparations for service abroad. The Home Guard protected vital establishments and installations, bridges, grid systems, and public utilities, and, prior to the formation of the R.A.F. Regiment, provided some of the defence for airfields. Eventually the Home Guard even provided gun crews for anti-aircraft defence and manned important coastal defences.

In many respects the Home Guard was an important training ground for young recruits waiting to be called up to the colours, and also relieved some of the strain on the police and the civil defence services during heavy air attacks. Home Guards assisting with rescue work and other air raid duties suffered many casualties.

Among the various Home Guard training centres established throughout Britain early in the war was one at Osterley Park, Middlesex, which attracted a lot of attention in the Press because tactics were being taught by Catalonian veterans of the recent Spanish Civil War, and a bemused Tom Wintringham, who had commanded a British battalion of the International Brigades. Volunteers at Osterley

42

Park were taught how to fight a guerrilla war in enemy-occupied territory, techniques in street fighting, and how to disable tanks with Molotov cocktails. From July 1940 until the Government took over in October, five thousand Home Guards passed through the school.

Relations between the Home Guard and the Forces were never too cordial. When the Home Guard were issued with regular serge battledress, greatcoats, and even duffel coats, steel helmets, and service respirators, the Army resented it. When they were issued with Tommy guns and the latest type of rifles, soldiers commented sarcastically, "They're beginning to look like real soldiers."

The Home Guard did in fact perform many duties of ordinary soldiers: they did suffer casualties and they did earn decorations. Although they earned no battle honours this was doubtless because of lack of opportunity. It seemed that the average Home Guard delighted far more in his role than did the average civilian called up into the services. Possibly the Home Guard was helped by the knowledge that he was not forced to live away from home, that he did not face the prospect of overseas service, or perhaps that he did not have to suffer fools unquestioningly as did members of the Armed Forces.

The bands played on

BY THE MIDDLE OF 1941 OUR BATTALION BOASTED A FIRST-CLASS band made up of twenty-three officers and men. Sometimes after we had been on a route march the band would meet us and play us back into camp. I must admit that I liked marching to the music of a band. But besides playing on ceremonial occasions, the band performed at social functions such as dances, gave concerts, and provided drummers and buglers for various other duties. An idea of what the band meant to our battalion is contained in this short item that appeared in the *Royal Fusiliers' Chronicle* in 1942.

We have had six weeks of camp and have just commenced battalion training. It was a very enjoyable camp, except for the bad weather.

Several Band concerts were held in the N.A.A.F.I. tent and thoroughly enjoyed by all. This is an excellent method of discovering hidden talent, and the work of impromptu turns would certainly contribute to a future Battalion concert party.

The General recently inspected the Battalion, subsequently taking the salute at the march-past. He seems very impressed with all he saw.

We are now back to our original billets and are finding the entertainments are as numerous as before. A very good Battalion All-Ranks Dance was recently held. This was in the nature of a farewell dance, so that we could in a measure entertain the many people who have been so kind to us down in these parts. Companies have also had their small but enjoyable farewell shows, and the Band has, as usual, been in great demand for these functions and has put up an excellent show of entertainments for them.

Bandmaster Quick, who had been bandmaster of the 1st Battalion in India prior to the war, was justifiably very proud of this band, which he had brought up to a high standard despite the fact that the bandsmen were always liable to be called on to perform their normal duties as soldiers.

Ann Miller.

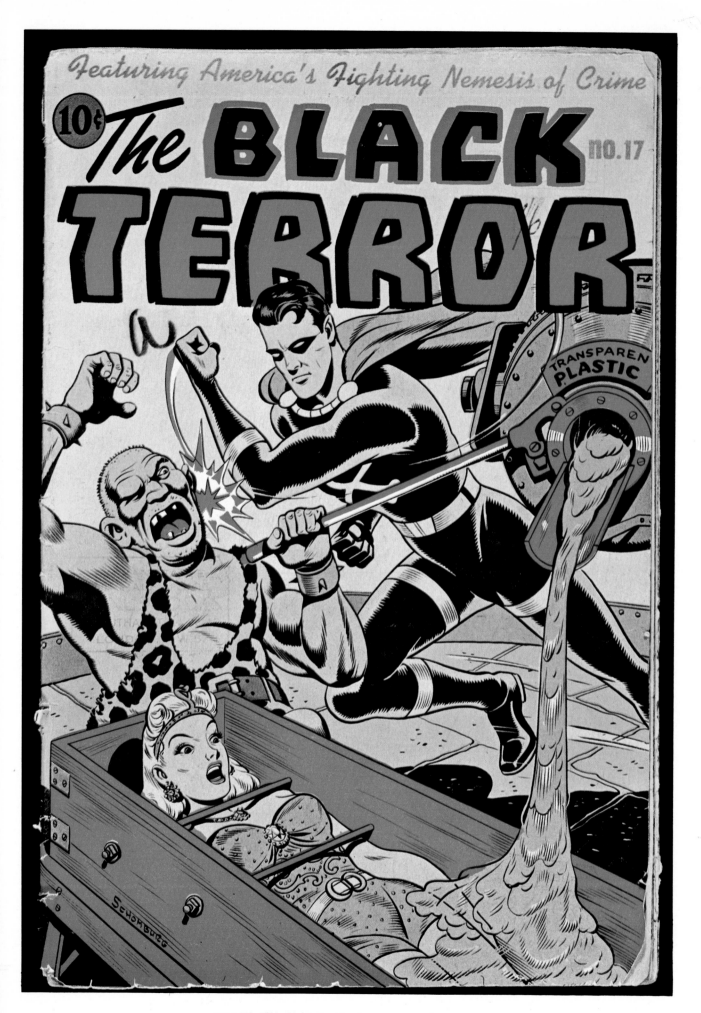

An American comic book of
1946.

An R.A.F. dance band in the early forties.

I remember coming back early one morning to Westward Ho! in Devon, from Exeter, where we had been to pick up rations, and a group of men were gathered round the back of the cookhouse. They were discussing a particularly heavy air raid on London the previous night. The West Indian bandleader Ken "Snakehips" Johnson and his tenor saxophonist, Dave Williams, had been among the many killed when a bomb had scored a direct hit on the Café de Paris, Piccadilly, where they were playing to a packed house. Ken's brother was a bandsman in our regimental band. Later it was said that looters had plundered the dead and dying, snatching jewellery and wristwatches and removing wallets and the contents of handbags.

Some months later while on leave, I was with my wife at the old Paramount Ballroom in Tottenham Court Road when the bandleader announced that the air raid siren had sounded. He resumed playing. The ballroom was in the basement of a block of flats, Paramount Court, and people from the flats began drifting down to shelter in the ballroom. As we came off the dance floor, we were surprised to see the mother and two sisters of a friend of mine who was away serving as an R.A.F. navigator, and we joined them at their table. It grew late and the raid grew more violent. There was no point in leaving as, according to an air raid warden, there were no trains.

45

The band continued to play, pausing only for short rest intervals. When a heavy blast shook the building, the lights went out for a while and we danced by candlelight. It was all very romantic, but I was beginning to feel hungry. My friends said that there was plenty of food in their flat on the top floor, so I begged them to let me have the key. The lift was not working, and I dashed up the stairs to the flat, where I grabbed a teacloth and filled it with nearly every bit of food I could find.

By now the building was shaking with the shock of almost incessant gunfire and exploding bombs, and I went up the one flight of stairs to the roof to see what was happening. As I looked down Tottenham Court Road, fires seemed to be blazing everywhere, and debris was strewn across the roadway. The peculiar pulsating sound of enemy aircraft engines could be heard despite the gunfire. London looked a sorry sight. I bolted down to the ballroom with my teacloth full of goodies, and we had a middle-of-the-night feast.

Dawn was breaking by the time the all-clear sounded, and only then did the band stand down. It is galling not to be able to recall the name of that band, which was magnificent.

With the likelihood that massive air attacks on Great Britain would follow the outbreak of war it had seemed downright foolish to allow concentrations of people to gather at places of entertainment. However, there was another grim possibility that worried the owners of cinemas, hotels, restaurants, and dance halls even more: that patrons would stay away even if they kept open for business, and they would lose more money. It was a chilling prospect.

But as the months passed, the British Expeditionary Force in France were hardly involved in active warfare, their French allies were engaged in just a few desultory skirmishes, and the dreaded air raids had not in fact materialized. People at home began to grow bored and restless. It was soon obvious even to the most obtuse authorities that entertainment for the services, war-workers, and even those going about their prosaic daily tasks, was vital for the maintenance of morale. So, as the "phoney war" extended into 1940, places of entertainment were reopened. Soon dance bands were playing to thousands at hotels, restaurants, and dance halls up and down the country, and, of course, band music continued to be broadcast.

Bands went to France to entertain bored base troops and to relieve the monotony of troops in the line waiting for the Germans or the Allies to fire the starting gun that would set the tanks rolling. The first leader to take his band to France was Jack Payne, who commenced his tour with a concert on Christmas Day, 1939, and returned to Britain in February 1940. While in France, Jack was forthright in his criticism of the poor quality of entertainment provided by NAAFI for British troops. His opinion was endorsed by practically everyone in the services.

In January 1940, Carroll Gibbons, who had been on holiday in the U.S.A. when the war broke out, managed to return to Britain

The Squadronaires at a reception.

despite the many difficulties. He opened at the Savoy Hotel with an eleven-piece band, and broadcast regularly throughout the war. He had a large following which appreciated his distinctive style and his staccato piano-playing. Joe Loss was over in France early in 1940 to play for the B.E.F., and in April 1940, Jack Hylton went to Paris to present concerts at the Opera House.

With the German invasion of Norway, the period of the "phoney war" was drawing to a close, and in May the long-expected *Blitzkrieg* began with the German onslaught on the Low Countries and France. By the end of June, Holland, Belgium, and France were finished and Britain faced the black prospect of invasion. It seemed that the only good thing was the weather, and people were not too sure about that for it might be ideal for German plans.

It was in June 1940 that the popular Lew Stone opened at the Dorchester with a seven-piece group, and he stayed there until June 1942, making frequent broadcasts. After leaving the Dorchester he formed a larger band, and for the rest of the war toured all over Britain playing at military camps, dance halls, and theatres. When he opened at the Glasgow Playhouse Ballroom for a three-week stint he played to a capacity house of thousands. And as the war was drawing to a close in Europe he was still packing them in at a hotel in Southampton. From 1947 to 1949, Lew Stone led the theatre orchestra for the hit show *Annie Get Your Gun*, and in the autumn of 1948 he was back on the air once again.

Ambrose, one of the most outstanding and successful bandleaders of pre-war years, lost many of his key bandsmen to the R.A.F. in March 1940. Most of them became members of the famous R.A.F. band, the Squadronaires. Ambrose managed to maintain a band, however, augmenting his group from studio orchestras in order to make recordings. He played at the Mayfair Hotel throughout the London blitz, which started in September 1940, but had to terminate his engagement because of ill health. Later, he formed an octet and continued to play and record for Decca.

Because of age and health reasons most well-known bandleaders were not called up for military service. But conscription did make inroads into their personnel, and the leaders had difficulty in maintaining their bands when their key players were called up. But their loss was the services' gain. Band musicians were organized into service bands, the most famous of these being the R.A.F. number one dance band, known to servicemen and -women in every theatre of war as the Squadronaires.

Squadron Leader O'Donnell, who was leader of the R.A.F. Central Band at Uxbridge, first thought of the idea of forming a first-class dance band, and he suggested to Les Brannelly that as the call-up would include many leading dance band musicians, they should be posted together to the R.A.F. to form an orchestra to entertain service personnel. Enthusiastic about the idea, Brannelly got together with other members of the Ambrose band and put the idea into operation. Initially the personnel included George Chisholm, Tommy McQuater, Harry Lewis, Andy McDevitt, Ronnie Aldrich, Jock Cummings, Jimmy Miller, and Sid Colin; but Eddie Breeze, Archie Craig, Kenny Baker, Monty Levy, Tommy Bradbury, Jimmy Durant, and others also played for the Squadronaires.

Before long the band was broadcasting regularly and it was acclaimed by critics and public alike. It continued to broadcast throughout the war. The Squadronaires made a public appearance at the London Coliseum in the "Dance Music Festival of 1942", and in 1943 the band was featured in a film, *The Life and Death of Colonel Blimp*. After the war the band continued to operate and was playing on the Continent until it was demobilized in 1946. The musicians decided to carry on in "civvy street". For a time their future seemed uncertain, but with fairly frequent broadcasts the band managed to survive and it was not until 1964 that the Squadronaires finally stood down.

During the war the band recorded for Decca as the Royal Air Force Dance Orchestra, but later its records were issued under the name the Squadronaires. Among their many recordings a Ronnie Aldrich arrangement of Spike Hughes' "Donegal Cradle Song" and "Jeepers Creepers" were outstanding.

No. 1 Balloon Centre Dance Orchestra, better known as the Skyrockets, was formed in 1940 at Blackpool, where a number of professional musicians were being trained as balloon riggers. In those days square pegs were still being knocked into round holes, but in this case not for long. The musicians were transferred to No. 1 Balloon Centre at Kidbrooke near London, and playing together as a band during their off-duty periods came to the notice of the Air Ministry, which had the good sense to take the band over. For the next two years the

Jimmy Dorsey (centre) with vocalists Helen O'Connell and Bob Eberly.

band was used for a series of inspired propaganda broadcasts directed at Hitler's *Luftwaffe*.

By 1942 the band's reputation was established. The Skyrockets appeared in the annual Jazz Jamboree and played their first public concert at the Colston Hall, Bristol. Until he was posted to another station the bandleader was George Beaumont. Thereafter, for the greater part of its existence, the leader was Paul Fenhoulet, a trombonist-arranger who before the war had worked with Carroll Gibbons at the Savoy Hotel. The band really came into its own when Balloon Command was scrapped and the Skyrockets found themselves in Fighter Command, receiving official recognition for the first time as a service band. The Skyrockets made a number of public appearances, but their popularity was mainly due to their frequent broadcasts and the recordings they made for Rex and Parlophone.

Like the Squadronaires, the band continued to function in the difficult post-war period. The Skyrockets became the pit orchestra for the show *High Time* at the London Palladium. After a disagreement about the musical direction, Paul Fenhoulet left in 1947, to be succeeded by Woolf Phillips. The band continued uneventfully at the Palladium through most of 1948, during which time they supported a show by Danny Kaye. The Skyrockets disbanded in 1950.

The Blue Rockets were an Army band formed by Eric Robinson for the Royal Army Ordnance Corps. When he was transferred to

49

Tommy Dorsey and his
band in a film of the forties.

the Army Radio Unit, the band came under the direction of Eric
Tann, the trombonist who had worked with Lew Stone, Henry Hall,
and Roy Fox. Eric continued working with the Blue Rockets until
he was invalided out of the Army in 1943. Early in 1942 the band
had received a recording contract with H.M.V., and this continued.

The Navy had its Blue Mariners led by George Crow, and Fighter
Command's own band included Kenny Baker, trumpeter, and Joe
Crossman and Aubrey Franks, saxophonists. There was a Bomber
Command Orchestra, an Ack Ack Band stationed in Scotland, and
even a London Fire Service Band. Many other units, such as the
Royal Fusiliers and the Royal Corps of Signals, had their own bands
which did a first-rate job in providing much-needed entertainment
for the troops and helping to boost morale, as well as functioning
as regimental or station bands for concerts, ceremonials, and even
on the march.

Nevertheless, newspapers sniped at bandsmen from time to time
when news was hard to come by and there was nobody else in parti-
cular to snipe at. In 1940 a press campaign had been conducted

50

against musicians, accusing them of trying to dodge military service, and now and again a musician of foreign extraction would be singled out for special treatment just to show that even though there was a war on the Press could still find space for the gossip and scandal so loved by a large section of the public.

Early in 1942 it was the turn of musicians already in the services to suffer a sustained press campaign, and they were sneeringly referred to as "chocolate" or "toy" soldiers. Such is the power of a smear campaign that even with a war on the authorities felt compelled to take action, and the disbandment of the Blue Rockets was the result. However, a month after the hullabaloo had died down and the newspapers had found something else to turn into copy, the band was quietly re-formed. It subsequently made broadcasts, recordings, and several public appearances.

In 1941 it was back to regular nightly dancing to resident bands at many West End hotels and restaurants. All over the country show business was booming. People were packing dance halls, and service-men and -women were some of the best customers although there were proprietors who complained that service boots were ruining their floors. Many servicemen carried shoes to wear at dances in respirator cases. Geraldo, whose band was always prominent during the war years, was appointed supervisor of the ENSA Band Division, touring the Middle East, North Africa, and Italy. After the war he continued to lead his orchestra but in addition ran an agency supply-ing entertainment groups for liners and pit orchestras for theatre circuits.

After the war the dance band scene in Britain began to drift. Few bands made headway in the new period of austerity. Notable exceptions were Billy Cotton's and Johnny Dankworth's, but the major band of the late forties was undoubtedly Ted Heath's, a jazz-type band that achieved wide success in Europe and America.

In the United States dance bands and swing bands were riding the crest of the wave in the early forties, with vocalists gradually achieving recognition and fame which sometimes exceeded that of the bands which featured them. Jimmy Dorsey left his brother Tommy to front his own band in 1941, and as a result of a recording of "Green Eyes" featuring a vocal duet by Eberly and O'Connell Jimmy's band hit the jackpot. This success was followed by a Johnny Mercer number, "Tangerine", which came to Britain and raged like a forest fire – possibly because of a nostalgic yearning for citrus fruits that were no longer obtainable in embattled Britain.

All the same, in Europe Jimmy's band never quite equalled the popularity of Tommy's, which was more of a swing band. Tommy scored a big hit with his recording of "I'm Getting Sentimental over You", and when young Frank Sinatra joined the band as a vocalist he was featured prominently in recordings with Tommy's vocal group, the Pied Pipers, and scored an overwhelming success with numbers such as "I'll Never Smile Again", "Hear My Song, Violetta", and

"Oh, Look At Me Now". Sinatra stayed with Tommy Dorsey until the summer of 1942.

Of all the big bands from America that enriched the world of dance music and helped sustain the morale of the Allies in the drab war years, the one with the deepest appeal was the band of Glenn Miller, whose style of music is still universally appreciated. In 1943 Miller organized his famous American Air Force Band and its success was practically instantaneous.

After a gruelling tour of the United States, Glenn came to Britain in the spring of 1944. He played to service audiences all over the country, and civilians who heard his broadcasts immediately took to the new sound: Every one of Miller's recordings was a success, and for many people nostalgic memories of World War II are conjured up by Miller's "Tuxedo Junction", "Pennsylvania 6-5000", "Chatanooga Choo Choo", and "American Patrol".

As the Allies were rolling up the Germans on the Continent, Glenn Miller was scheduled to go to France and take his band on an extensive tour of the Western Front. In December 1944, Glenn Miller and three others left England to fly to Paris to finalize arrangements for the tour. The plane took off from an airfield in southern England and flew into thick fog over the English Channel, to disappear without trace.

Today Glenn Miller is a legend. In the world of music, which has since been assaulted with a variety of sounds from bop to pop, it is not surprising that the Glenn Miller sound still works its magic.

Remember Pearl Harbor!

AN UNCLE OF MINE WHO HAD A SMALL IMPORT AND EXPORT company in Manhattan was in Honolulu on business in December 1941. Intending to take it easy on Sunday, December 7, he was in bed asleep when the Japanese struck at Oahu.

He said that he woke to the sound of muffled explosions which he knew instinctively came from the direction of Hickam Field and Pearl Harbor, America's key air and sea bases in the Pacific, and he thought, "What the hell?" Practice, manoeuvres, or whatever seemed a bloody cheek on a peaceful Sunday morning. But soon he realized that there was a lot of coming and going in the hotel corridor outside and the sound of explosions and gunfire seemed too sustained and a little too realistic to be manoeuvres. Then the penny dropped. "Japs!" he thought, "who else?"

He dressed quickly and went downstairs to the hotel lobby. People were crowding round the entrance and looking east towards Hickam and Pearl. Columns of smoke could be seen in the distance billowing slowly into the early morning sky, and already a smell of burning could be detected in the air. My uncle joined one group of bewildered people and took part in the excited speculation and gossip about what was happening. Suddenly there was the dull boom of a tremendous explosion and a tremor ran through the ground. Conversation ceased just for a few seconds in the lull that followed the ominous explosion. A little later a delivery man shouted that the Japs had landed and were knocking the hell out of Pearl Harbor, whereupon my uncle decided it was time for breakfast. He found that the breakfast lounge was empty, so he went to the kitchen. Nobody was around, so he helped himself to coffee and rolls, put the lot on a tray, and went to a table on the terrace.

He had no idea what to do, nor, it seemed, did anyone else for that matter. While he was considering the situation there came more heavy explosions and the sound of anti-aircraft guns. Seconds later an explosion which seemed to have come from no more than a block away shook the building. People standing around in the hotel lobby disappeared like magic in all directions, but were back within minutes to hear a news bulletin on the radio. It was brief and merely mentioned that a sporadic air attack had been made on Oahu.

A passing truck slowed down outside the hotel, and the driver called out that a lot of people had been killed or wounded and the hospitals were crowded. It was terrible, he said, and if he were them he would get the hell away from the city because the Japs, the Germans, or the Russians would soon be bombing the hell out of it. "But where to go?" asked everybody. "Where are the enemy? Why does nobody tell us anything?"

My uncle decided to take a walk and see if he could learn something about what was actually going on that morning. More explosions! One or two sounded close. A policeman told my uncle to get off the street if he did not wish to be machine-gunned down by Jap planes, but the policeman did not appear to be very sure of what he was saying. My uncle picked up a newspaper at a newsstand. The newspapers were right on the ball with headlines that read: WAR! JAPANESE BOMB OAHU.

Back to the hotel went my uncle. By the time he reached it the anti-aircraft fire had stopped, but there were still occasional muffled explosions from the direction of Pearl Harbor. My uncle packed an overnight bag. It seemed the only thing to do at the time, he said.

During the course of the day rumour followed rumour: bombs had fallen downtown; the Lewers and Cooke Building had been completely demolished; hospitals were so crowded with casualties that they were unable to cope; the fleet at anchor in Pearl had been wiped out; over two hundred Japanese planes had been shot down; the Japanese had established a bridgehead at Haleiwa; Japanese and German paratroops had landed between Schofield Barracks and Wheeler Field. There were further rumours of seaborne landings in the north following a naval bombardment by a Japanese fleet; of Japanese fifth-columnists sabotaging planes and trucks, sniping at Army and Navy personnel, and destroying telephone communications. A persistent rumour that Japanese fifth-columnists had poisoned water supplies so scared many people that they refrained from drinking water until impelled by thirst and the realization that nobody who had drunk water seemed to suffer any ill-effects.

After a while everyone seemed to settle down. They listened to the radio bulletins, the music in between, and the announcer breaking in occasionally to relay orders to military and naval units. That night, except for a blackout, the occasional crack of a rifle or pistol shot, and the fact that many servicemen had vanished from the streets, hotels, and bars, it was dinner and drinks more or less as usual.

The sparkle had suddenly gone out of Honolulu, but the mood did not last long. According to my uncle, the Americans felt that although they had been caught with their pants down, in the end it would be the Japs who would lose theirs.

The events of those fateful hours, which brought America into the war, were as follows. At 0755 hours on December 7, 1941, a solitary dive-bomber swooped down over Ford Island in the middle of Pearl Harbor and released a bomb which struck a seaplane ramp. Pulling out of its dive, it went streaking low over the channel between the island and the warships packing the docks on the mainland. Two more planes immediately followed through and scored hits on the American Navy's PBY hangars. Over Pearl City a group of five planes circled lazily, then split up and headed towards the line of ships anchored off the north-west side of Ford Island. Two sped unerringly towards the old battleship *Utah*, one towards the old cruiser *Raleigh*, and one towards another old cruiser, the *Detroit*, just ahead. Perplexed Navy men, unsure whether this was a genuine attack or realistic battle practice, were rushing to take up action stations when the planes launched torpedoes, veered, and soared off across the channel. The *Raleigh* lurched violently as a great grout of an orange-tinted mixture of oily smoke and mud heaved from its side.

The *Utah*, struck squarely by a brace of torpedoes, shook from stem to stern, and timber on deck used as a shield in practice bombing began to slip over the side. The *Detroit* and the *Tangier* astern of the *Utah* were, for the moment, unharmed. The fifth plane flew right across Ford Island, across the channel, and over the *California*, and let loose a torpedo in the general direction of the old minelayer *Oglala* and the *Helena*, which were moored side by side at Ten-Ten Dock.

The torpedo passed right under the *Oglala* and rammed into the *Helena* amidships. The violence of the explosion not only crippled the *Helena* but burst the seams of the *Oglala* and strewed debris across the dock. Aboard the *Helena* seamen worked hard to check water pouring through the damaged drain system, and topside, where the fo'c'sle had been wrecked, men tried to bring up ammunition for anti-aircraft guns. To the starboard, the *Oglala* was listing heavily and beginning to sink. Tugs doggedly made their way to the scene to tow the vessel clear of the *Helena* and give the cruiser's newly installed 1.1 guns a chance to go into action.

On the other side of Ford Island, at the northern end of Battleship Row, the band was assembled on the deck of the *Nevada* waiting to play morning colours at 0800 hours. The men shifted uneasily as the heavy crump of an explosion then another reverberated across the channel. Then as the band struck up "The Star-spangled Banner" a Japanese plane swooped across the channel and loosed a torpedo at the warship next in line, the *Arizona*, then soared off over the *Nevada*, machine-gunning the deck.

By now all over the harbour men were swarming to take up action stations, but the surprise had been complete. Within seconds the line of battleships along Battleship Row were nothing more than target ships for the swift-striking Japanese. The *Oklahoma* alongside the inboard *Maryland* was struck by the first of five torpedoes; the *West Virginia* alongside the *Tennessee* received the first of six, and the *Arizona* caught two.

After the attack – scene in a
Honolulu street.

In came the Japanese again. Four more torpedoes ripped the *Okla-homa* apart. All lights went out below decks, and the trapped crewmen groped frenziedly towards ladders and companionways to get topside as the ship started to heel over. Equipment and fixtures broke loose. Huge rolls of steel towing cable trundled across the decks, bowling over men trying to reach the ladders, and in the handling room thousand-pounder shells careered crazily across the deck sending men sprawling. Then with a terrifying shudder the ship keeled over and turned turtle. Some men on deck managed to scramble with the roll of the ship across the side and onto the upended bottom. Others were flung into the sea. Many men were trapped inside the hull. Thirty-two survivors were cut loose by rescue workers more than thirty hours later.

Bombs as well as torpedoes scored hits on the helpless warships. The *Arizona* was struck repeatedly by heavy bombs, one of which shattered the boat deck. The *Vestal* alongside her was struck by a bomb which fell through an open hatch, tore through the bowels of the ship and through the bottom, and then exploded. The ship shook and almost jumped from the water. The sea poured relentlessly into the holds and the vessel started to go down by the stern.

The *Maryland* took on men from the capsized ship, but, too hope-lessly placed to put up any sustained fire power to discourage the Japanese from swooping across Battleship Row, was lucky to be hit by only two bombs. One hit the fo'c'sle, showering the deck with

splintered wreckage and fragmented plates; the other tore into the hull
below the waterline.

Anti-aircraft guns on shore as well as aboard ships were sending up
a barrage of fire, but undeterred, the Japanese planes went mercilessly
about their business. The *Nevada* was hit by a torpedo as her machine-
gunners did what they could to keep the enemy at bay. The ship was
already listing to port when she was struck by another bomb.

A Japanese torpedo plane scored a hit on the *West Virginia*, and as
she lurched and rolled, bombs burst on deck and several more torpedoes struck home. The ship listed steeply, and in the holds and
lower decks men tried desperately to get aloft. Thick yellow smoke
swirled and eddied through the holds. Oil seeped into the lower decks,
drenching the struggling sailors. In key positions aboard the ship
other men worked hard to control the situation by counterflooding;
they succeeded in bringing the *West Virginia* slowly back to starboard,
and she finally settled on the harbour bottom on an even keel.

Moored on her own, further down Battleship Row just ahead of the
tanker *Neosho*, was the battleship *California*. Within ten minutes of the
start of the raid she was struck by several torpedoes, and the sea
flooded in, rupturing fuel tanks and putting the power plant out of
commission. Fires started on board and the ship began to sink, but
many of the crew stuck to their guns, blazing away defiantly at the low-
flying Japanese planes.

Men were still struggling in the oily water between the wreck of the
Oklahoma and the *Maryland* when the *Arizona* blew up. The concussion
surged across Ford Island and the channel as a gigantic flaming ball
blossomed into the air in a mushroom of billowing black oily smoke.
The stunning hurricane of disturbed air hurled crewmen from the
decks of the *Nevada*, the *Vestal*, and the *West Virginia*. The awesome
sight of the atomized battleship could be seen by everyone all over
Pearl Harbor and for miles around. In a flash one thousand men

A Japanese plane peels off after scoring a direct hit on the *Oklahoma*.

disappeared forever. Yet miraculously there were men who lived through the inferno and struggled to reach some place on the red-hot deck to launch themselves into the oily waters.

As the *Arizona* blew up, the repair ship *Vestal*, moored alongside, lurched sickeningly. Blast devastated the superstructure and swept men from the deck. But crewmen moving swiftly into action managed to cut loose the hawsers linking the *Vestal* to the blazing *Arizona*, and a Navy tug towed the battered little ship to safety.

The *Tennessee*, moored inboard of the *West Virginia*, was struck by two armour-piercing bombs. Jagged hunks of metal were hurled across to the *West Virginia*, one searing into the bridge, fatally wounding Captain Mervyn Bennion in the stomach.

On the other side of Ford Island, the *Detroit* and the *Tangier* were still intact; but lying between them the *Utah* was listing heavily, and the *Raleigh* had suffered extremely heavy damage, although her anti-aircraft guns continued to engage the enemy.

At Ten-Ten Dock and in berths beyond, ships which could have engaged the enemy stood by helplessly as the raiders soared back and forth across the channel practically without hindrance. The *Sacramento* had just come out of dry dock and her ammunition lockers had not been refilled. The *Swan* was undergunned, although she did all she could with just two serviceable three-inch guns. The *Rigel*, the *Ramapo*, and the *New Orleans* were without ammunition. The *San Francisco*, which was in the process of being overhauled, had all her guns in the workshops and her ammunition in store ashore.

The *St. Louis* and the *Honolulu* were in not much better straits. In Drydock No. 1, south of the *Oglala* and the *Helena* off Ten-Ten Dock, the battleship *Pennsylvania* and the destroyers *Cassin* and *Downes*, which it hemmed in, had not yet been attacked, and the men did what they could to meet the Japanese onslaught which they felt was sure to come.

In the harbour south of Pearl City, the aircraft tender *Curtiss*, moored offshore, waited for orders to move while the seamen watched the devastation taking place off Ford Island. But the destroyer *Helen* had been ready to move, and not long after the attack started she went speeding down the channel through the torpedo nets, which had not been closed, and out of the harbour, where she spotted a Japanese midget submarine on the coral. The *Helen* opened fire, but failing to hit the sub she took up patrol of the harbour entrance.

Off Pearl City, first a destroyer-minelayer, then the repair ship *Medusa* and the *Curtiss*, spotted the conning tower of a submarine and signalled the destroyer *Monaghan*. The *Curtiss* put a shell through the conning tower, and the submarine replied by firing two torpedoes. One just missed the *Curtiss*, and the other sped by the *Monaghan* and exploded on the shore of Ford Island. The *Monaghan* then tried to ram the submarine and missed, but a few well-placed depth charges smashed the Japanese midget to the bottom, nearly wrecking the *Downes* into the bargain.

The second wave of the Japanese attack began at 0840 hours, with eighty dive-bombers and thirty-six fighters concentrating on Pearl Harbor, and fifty-four high-level bombers making for Hickam Field and Kaneohe. This time, fortunately, there were no torpedo bombers in the attacking forces. As the Japanese dived on Pearl, the Americans opened up with every available gun in an effort to drive off the raiders.

Incredibly, the *Nevada*, a battleship which normally needed two and a half hours to fire her boilers and four tugs to pull and turn her, started to move off and drift away with the tide, swinging clear of the still burning *Arizona*. But the Japanese did not intend to leave the ship sailing down the channel unmolested. A flight of dive-bombers switched their attack from the *Helena* to strike at the moving battleship instead. More planes swooped on the *Nevada*. Wreathed in smoke, belching flames, and racked by explosions, the ship ploughed on. It was struck by bombs again and again.

The *Nevada* was well down the channel and was passing Ten-Ten Dock when she found half the channel blocked by a pipeline stretching from Ford Island to the dredger *Turbine*. Quartermaster Sedbury coolly took the *Nevada* through the gap, passing the *Shaw* in the floating dry dock. But signals from ashore to the *Nevada* ordered her to cut her engines. The risk of the warship sinking and blocking the channel was too great. As the ship swung round in the wind and current and prepared to drop anchor, Japanese bombers roared in for a final attempt to scupper her and three bombs fell just off her bow.

The Japanese next turned their attention to the *Pennsylvania*, the *Cassin*, and the *Downes*, cramped in Drydock No. 1. Bombs rained down around the dock, some falling on buildings in the Navy Yard. The *Pennsylvania* was hit, but her guns went on firing. Bombs crashed on the *Cassin* and the *Downes*, and soon fierce fires were raging aboard both ships. A big explosion tore the *Cassin* apart, and heeling over heavily to starboard she rolled over on the *Downes*, pressing her against the side of the dry dock. Then a bomb plunged into the flooding dry dock, adding to the chaos in the Navy Yard area.

Commander Shin-Ichi Shimuzu, who organized supplies for the raid. Commander Mitsuo Fuchida, leader of the Japanese pilots in the raid.

Over in the floating dry dock, the *Shaw* was struck by a bomb, starting a fire that spread rapidly towards the powder magazine. Then the ship erupted into a showering volcano in a spectacular explosion that took away the breath of everyone who witnessed it. From the billows of reddish and black smoke, fragments of white-hot metal and shell casings trailing tenuous streamers of white smoke rocketed into the sky and curved away, raining debris in all directions.

To the north, off Pearl City, a damaged Japanese plane plunged into the deck of the *Curtiss*, starting a big fire. Dive-bombers swooping down for the kill rained bombs on the aircraft tender, scoring hits. One bomber as it veered away loosed two bombs, one of which struck the *Raleigh*, tearing through the decks and the bottom of the ship and exploding in the silt below. The *Raleigh* listed heavily to port. Crewmen worked feverishly to clear the top deck in an effort to prevent the ship from capsizing. As the planes flew off, over the side of the ship went everything that could be moved, from torpedo tubes and torpedoes to ladders, chains, and stanchions. Pumps were brought in from the Navy Yard, and even one from the *Medusa* was brought across the channel. Holes were plugged with blankets, life-jackets, and canvas, and wreckage was cut loose and tossed over the side. Meanwhile the *Raleigh's* guns kept firing.

Further to the north the tender *Dobbin*, moored with her five destroyers, suffered casualties and damage to her superstructure when a bomb exploded just off her starboard side. Some distance between the *Dobbin* and the *Allen* was the hospital ship *Solace*, where a stream of launches and small vessels moved back and forth ferrying wounded from the stricken ships in Battleship Row. Some destroyers, although without their skippers, who had not been able to get back to their boats from ashore when the attack started, were now moving

61

The *Arizona* explodes after a direct hit by a bomb.

past the *Solace* and down Battleship Row making for the harbour entrance and the open sea. The *Monaghan*, the *Dale*, the *Blue*, the *Henley*. the *Phelps*, and the *Aylwin* reached the open sea about an hour after the Japanese had struck their first blow.

Men aboard the *Honolulu* and the *St. Louis*, tied up alongside a pier in the Navy Yard, were trying to cast off the lines between them when a bomb smashed through a concrete pier and exploded near the port side of the *Honolulu*. Damage to her oil tanks and the buckling of her plates effectively stopped any hope of her making a sortie. A power line to the dock was fractured, putting out all lights and rendering useless all electrical gear needed to power the guns. On the opposite side of the pier, the *New Orleans* suffered a similar fate and ammunition had to be manhandled from the magazines to the guns.

Japanese bomber's view of Battleship Row: oil gushes from the *Oklahoma* and the *West Virginia* while astern the *Arizona* has been hit by a bomb.

62

The *Arizona* on fire after the great explosion.

Aboard the cruiser *St. Louis* berthed on the outside of the *Honolulu*, sailors worked tirelessly to free their ship of the shackles that prevented her from putting to sea. A jammed gangway was burned away with a blow-torch, the thick water hose to the shore was chopped loose, and ropes and hawsers cast off. Just after 0930 hours the *St. Louis* began backing out into the channel. Men who had been ashore on liberty when the attack started were still trying to rejoin their ship even as the last Japanese raider wheeled away to sea. At that moment the *Oglala* gave up the ghost and rolled over.

In Battleship Row fires raged out of control on the *West Virginia*, and orders were given to abandon ship. Men dived over the side, swimming desperately to avoid patches of burning oil drifting down the channel. Some of the men trapped in the hull of the upside-down *Oklahoma* managed to get out through a porthole and reach safety. Meanwhile aboard the *California* Captain J. W. Bunkley also decided it was time to abandon ship as burning oil gathered round the stern. Men rushed to scramble ashore, but when the burning oil suddenly began to clear, the captain realized that there was a chance to save the ship after all and appealed to his men to return to fight the fires aboard. Some men did.

Men from the *Raleigh* and the *Tangier* with cutting apparatus arrived on the upturned *Utah* and began cutting through the hull where noises had been heard coming from within. It took an hour of gruelling work to cut a hole through the metal plates. One survivor, Fireman John Vaessen, came through.

Early that fateful Sunday morning, in the control tower of Hickam Field between Pearl Harbor and Honolulu, Colonel William

63

The *Arizona*—a tomb for 1,102 men.

Farthing was waiting for the B-17s due to arrive after their fourteen-hour flight from the mainland. As his eyes swept the skyline he saw a line of aircraft approaching from the north-west. He gave them no more than a passing glance as he scanned the sky for the B-17s. He thought they were Marine planes from Ewa Field.

Seconds later a plane dived on Hickam and released a bomb which hit the large hangar of the Hawaiian Air Depot. More planes came in from the south and roared across the airfield machine-gunning the rows of planes stacked neatly out in the open. Dive-bombers struck at the hangars, buildings, and airfield installations. As men rushed from barracks and living quarters to take up action stations, they were cut down in their tracks by Zero fighters swooping in from all angles.

Even as Hickam and Pearl heaved and rocked under the rain of bombs, another Japanese strike force rendezvoused near the Waianae Mountains. Minutes later the force swooped down on Wheeler Field, the Army base to the north between Pearl and Schofield. Here, too, the neat rows of planes were shot to pieces and hangars and barrack blocks blasted by bombs without the Americans being able to retaliate. Japanese planes flew low over the barrack blocks and parade grounds of Schofield. Someone sounded an air raid alarm, and men came tumbling out of the buildings hardly realizing what was going on. Some men rushed to take up their posts, but in the chaos and confusion little positive was done, and it was only after the Japanese had flown off that stock was taken and the Army wheels began to grind slowly in preparation for the anticipated further attacks.

To the west across the Koolau Mountains at Kaneohe Naval Air Station, Japanese planes came in low to strafe the hangars. American

Ensign Sakamaki commanded a midget submarine.

pilots raced by car for their planes hoping to be able to take off and engage the raiders, but by the time they reached the hangars not only were all twenty-six PBYs ablaze in their rows but four more moored in the bay had been destroyed together with many of the small craft that serviced them. Americans manned machine-guns and blazed away at the Japanese skimming over the trees. The planes wheeled away, but fifteen minutes later a squadron of Japanese bombers appeared flying in close formation. Bombs rained down on Kaneohe, wrecking hangars, barracks, and installations. The Japanese left the Naval Air Station a shambles. Only three PBYs out on patrol at the time of the attack were safe.

At Bellows Field, the Army fighter base only six miles down the coast from Kaneohe, a single Japanese plane skimmed down out of the blue firing its machine-guns and was gone almost immediately. Personnel on the base were puzzled but not particularly perturbed. A little while later, a B-17, one of the group from the mainland, which had not been able to land at Hickam Field, came in to land on the short runway. A squadron of Japanese fighters immediately behind peeled off and strafed the airfield. Three American pilots tried to get aloft to engage the raiders. One fell victim to six Zeros almost at once, another never got off the ground, and the third was hit as he took off. The pilot managed to bring his plane down in the sea and swim to safety.

At Ewa Field, the Marine base west of Pearl, two lines of torpedo bombers and three squadrons of Zero fighters came in from the west. Some of the Zeros peeled off and streaked towards the parked rows of fighters. Others selected hangars and buildings for their targets. Within minutes thirty-three of the forty-nine planes lined up on the field were destroyed. Not one got off the ground. There was no

Ensign Sakamaki's midget submarine beached off Bellows Field.

65

The *Nevada*, beached after the raid.

anti-aircraft defence, and for the Japanese criss-crossing the Marine base the attack was a cakewalk.

At John Rogers Airport, the civilian airfield, an inter-island flight to Maui was standing by ready to take off at 0800 hours when everyone was peremptorily ordered off the plane. The puzzled passengers returned to the terminal building, where they were told about the Japanese attack on the island. They were incredulous, but any doubts they may have had about the matter vanished as Japanese planes came sweeping in from the sea and strafed the airfield.

The B-17s due in from the mainland were twelve planes of the 38th and 88th Reconnaissance Squadrons, under Major Truman Landon. The planes had not been flying in formation but singly to save petrol on the long flight. They were unarmed and had been stripped of their armour to lighten them. Near Oahu a couple of the planes ran into Japanese fighters, but fortunately for them the Japanese were intent on conserving their ammunition for their major role and wasted none on the B-17s. Crews of the B-17s did not realize what was happening in Oahu even when they saw columns of smoke rising from the ground, and it was not until the rows of blazing planes and the devastated buildings at Hickam Field could be seen below that it began to dawn on the B-17 crews that something serious was amiss. They knew for sure seconds later as they tried to land. Japanese planes were still strafing the airfield. As the first of the B-17s touched down crews tumbled onto the tarmac and raced for cover. Fire tenders were hampered through lack of water due to fractured water-mains, and in any case it was perilous work trying to put out fires as the Japanese strafed anything that moved. Servicemen used small-arms and machine-guns in a futile effort to drive off the raiders. Some civilians headed away from the base for what they thought were safer areas, but for the next hour or two it appeared

The *Nevada* aground at
Hospital Point.

The destroyers *Cassin* and
Downes, wrecked in Drydock
No. 1.

that no place was safe from the attentions of the busy Japanese. Explosions seemed to be coming from every direction all over the island, and the inevitable rumours of Japanese landings were already beginning to spread to add to the alarm and confusion.

At Haleiwa Airfield two lieutenants, Welch and Taylor, had managed to get airborne in their P40s and were scanning the skies for the enemy. Their first victim – they claimed many more – was a Japanese Zero which crashed in a pineapple field. Two B-17s which had already tried to land at Wheeler, Ewa, and Hickam circled

The destroyer *Shaw* exploding in the floating dry dock.

The cruiser *St. Louis* passing the upturned hull of the *Oklahoma*.

to land on the short runway at Haleiwa. They managed to come in safely, but a Zero flew in firing at the airmen as they raced for cover. Fortunately the Japanese plane was short of ammunition and it zoomed away.

At Hickam mechanics worked frantically in damaged hangars to clear wrecks and try to make rapid repairs to one or two aircraft with minor damage in order to put them in the air to counter further Japanese attacks. Other personnel dashed hither and thither in a belated effort to organize some ground defence for the stricken field. Trenches were being dug and sandbagged emplacements were being set up when Japanese bombers came flying in in a V formation for a high level attack. Bombs whistled down and hangars and buildings

Ten-Ten Dock after the attack: the capsized *Oglala* and the torpedoed cruiser *Helena* on the left.

70

Rescue launches pick up survivors from the battleship *West Virginia*.

disintegrated. Soon the whole area was once again enveloped in clouds of choking dust and smoke as barracks and stores were hit. The mess hall was demolished and casualties were heavy. Service personnel and civilians cowered under any cover that seemed to offer some protection from the rain of steel, but most hope of protection was illusory. No preparations had been made to meet such air attacks.

At 0915 hours, the Japanese returned with dive-bombers to complete their work of destruction and were met by fire from machine-guns which had been hastily mounted for anti-aircraft defence. Bombs patterned the field with smoking craters, and more hits were scored on vital installations such as the underground petrol system and a water main. Volunteers flocked to the field from all quarters to assist the hardpressed airfield personnel and rescue workers while families of servicemen and civilian employees at the air base were evacuated.

As soon as the raiders had departed men worked strenuously to organize fresh defences against anticipated further attacks from the

Men swarm down the side of
the torpedoed *California* as
burning oil from the *Arizona*
engulfs her stern.

The only B-17 destroyed—
Captain Ray Swanson's aircraft at Hickam Field.

Raising the battleship
California in 1943.

Raising the *Oklahoma* in
1943.

73

The battleship *West Virginia* in service again in 1944.

air and by land. It was fully expected that the Japanese would try to capture the airfield where the runways and control tower had been left intact. More machine-gun emplacements and rifle pits were dug and manned. Food supplies were checked and made ready. At dusk sentries were posted, and as it became dark the sound of desultory shots fired by jumpy sentries could be heard, and sometimes a sustained fusillade would give substance to the rumours of Japanese landings which were rife.

All over the island there were few people who slept that night. Nobody doubted that the Japanese had not yet finished with Oahu. Nobody dreamed that the Japanese would never come back, no more than they had dreamed that they would come in the first place.

Surely there never could have been a more open and worthwhile naval target for an enemy than Pearl Harbor when the Japanese struck their shattering blow at the nerve centre of the American Pacific Fleet. Well over ninety American battleships, destroyers, submarines, tenders, and service craft were packed together in berths and docks or moored strung out at convenient intervals around the waters of the great harbour. On the airfield planes were neatly parked in rows in the open so that they could more easily be guarded against sabotage, a contingency that the Americans did anticipate.

Three hundred and fifty-three Japanese planes actually took part in the raid on Oahu, flying from carriers operating thousands of miles from their base. The damage they did exceeded anything the Japanese planners had thought possible, although they had hoped to find American aircraft carriers at Pearl. As it was, 18 American warships were sunk or crippled, 188 Army and Navy planes were destroyed, mostly on the ground, and another 159 were damaged.

In Honolulu damage to the extent of half a million dollars was done, all but one instance being the result of badly fused American anti-aircraft shells.

The Americans lost 2,403 killed, including 68 civilians. The Japanese killed amounted to about 170 men, and they lost 29 aircraft, a large submarine, and 5 midget submarines. The calculated Japanese gamble had paid handsome dividends, but as far as Hawaii was concerned it was a one-shot operation which, successful as it was for the Japanese, they were not able to repeat. For just two hours in World War II, Hawaii was a combat zone. They were two hours the Americans will never forget.

Arnhem – the Big Drop

I READ ABOUT THE BATTLE FOR ARNHEM WHILE I WAS IN SOUTH-East Asia, and I still remember the graphic, down-to-earth daily reports by Alan Wood, the *Daily Express* reporter on the spot. I also heard Stanley Maxted's on-the-spot broadcasts for the B.B.C. When Lieutenant-General F. A. M. ("Boy") Browning, Commander of the 1st Airborne Corps at the time of Arnhem (although not a participant in the battle), came out to the Far East, he gave a talk about the operations, but by then other things had happened and were still happening.

Some of the old battalion had transferred to Airborne as para-chutists and glider pilots, but except for a brief encounter with one or two of them after they had got their wings, I never heard any more about them. It is possible some of them were at Arnhem. I did meet a man after the war who had been with the 1st Airborne Division at Oosterbeek and had been awarded an M.M., but we did not talk about the war: we had other, more pressing things to talk about at the time.

I used to know a newspaper man in Amsterdam who had been living in Arnhem at the time the 1st Airborne Division dropped in. His father had been a courier for the Dutch Resistance, and an aunt had been a nurse at one of the hospitals. He himself had not witnessed the main landings, but he had seen paratroopers enter Arnhem. For a while it had seemed that all was going well; but before long the Germans recovered from their initial shock, and as the battle developed my acquaintance, like so many other Dutchmen in Arnhem, Oosterbeek, and surrounding villages, had been forced to spend a good deal of his time in a cellar hearing the din of battle, but seeing very little.

When the British had withdrawn and the battle was over, the news-man had seen British prisoners being marched away through the streets, some of them singing. He described the aftermath of the battle, the ruins of buildings, burned-out shops and houses, and streets littered with abandoned equipment, cartridge and shell cases, and other debris of battle. The hospitals were overflowing with wounded, British, German, and a number of Dutch, and German ambulances ran a shuttle-service to remove many of them to hospitals in the north. He told me that the Dutch had been bitterly disappointed at the outcome of the Airborne operations. When the British had come, there had been joy at first, then the sustained battle, the din and devastation, had brought uncertainty and fear. Finally the British were gone and the Germans were back. "It was," said the newsman wryly, "an unhappy time."

Not long after the war I saw a film of the Arnhem operations called *Theirs is the Glory*. It was made by Castleton Knight for J. Arthur Rank in 1946, when the ruins at Arnhem and Oosterbeek had not yet been cleared. Told in documentary style and acted by men who were there, the scenes were authentic and the action realistic. Now Richard Attenborough has directed the film of Cornelius Ryan's account of the battle for Arnhem, *A Bridge Too Far*.

I have read many books and accounts of Arnhem, including *A Bridge Too Far*, but the one that impressed me the most was *Arnhem* by Major-General R. E. Urquhart, C.B., D.S.O., who commanded the 1st Airborne Division in the operation. I have read his fascinating account over and over again; it is compulsive reading. General Urquhart, a big, well-built man, too heavy to be a parachutist, went into battle by glider. His restrained story, told simply yet with sharp detail, with candour and clarity, has the depth of feeling and compassion that only a man who was there, and who, in addition, had intimate knowledge of "befores" and "afters" of the operation, could express.

Like all battles, Arnhem was a different battle for every man who took part in it. To one it was a week of suffering lying wounded in an evil-smelling cellar; to another it was days of house-to-house fighting; and to yet another it was agonizing days in and out of slit trenches. But to every man who survived the battle one thing was certain: it had been sheer hell.

Sunday, September 17, 1944, was clear and fine as at airfields all over Southern England teams of men in net-covered crash helmets or red berets and camouflage smocks crowded around Dakotas, Stirlings, Halifaxes, and Horsa and giant Hamilcar gliders loaded with jeeps, seventeen-pounder anti-tank guns, and other heavy equipment. Soon paratroopers and glider-borne infantry, weighed down with accoutrements and extra equipment attached to arms, legs, and chest, climbed aboard their various aircraft and, having swallowed their anti-airsickness pills, settled down in discomfort for the long flight to Holland.

A force of 4,700 Allied aircraft had been assembled for Operation Market Garden, the code name for the invasion of Holland by British and American airborne divisions to seize bridges above Eindhoven, at Grave, at Nijmegen, and at Arnhem, and hold them until the British Second Army drove a wedge through the Germans to link up with the bridgeheads. The most distant objective was the bridge at Arnhem, and to the 1st Airborne Division was allotted the task of seizing and holding it for at least twenty-four hours until relieved.

The action started with over twelve hundred Allied bombers pounding German gun positions, approach roads, and railheads around the proposed dropping zones. After an uneventful flight over the North Sea, scores of aircraft carrying paratroopers, and towing gliders full of troops and equipment, crossed the flooded coast of Holland and nosed inland over the flat fields and meadows patched green and brown like the smocks worn by the airborne troops. Almost over Hertogenbosch, the force split up, the 1st Airborne heading north-east towards Arnhem, while the 82nd and 101st American Divisions made for Grave and Nijmegen.

The first landings in the vicinity of Arnhem were made by Major B. A. Wilson's Independent Company of tough, battle-tried paratroopers, which included twenty-five German-speaking Jewish ex-refugees. Their immediate job was to clear and mark out landing sites with strips of orange and red nylon fabric and to help with subsequent landings of men and supplies. Fifteen minutes later, the gliders came sailing in. Released from their tows, they came hurtling down at an alarming speed, ploughing and slewing across fields to pull up with a bone-jarring jolt. Some crashed into trees, others turned turtle; a few dropped like stones, splintering on the ground and hurling bodies in all directions. Men came tumbling out into the fields from dozens of gliders, some taking up firing positions and others dragging away guns, jeeps, handcarts, and other equipment. The fields were beginning to look like sites for the setting up of huge circuses.

A little while later Dakotas flew over low, spilling hundreds of parachutists, and their blue, red, and yellow parachuted supply cannisters, across the sky. Most of the men got down safely, although there were a number of "Roman candles" and messy landings. Curious civilians were beginning to appear on the scene, and some indicated that the Germans had made off in all directions, shocked out of their skins at the first approach of the roaring air armada. Some of the civilians were patients who had wandered away from a nearby mental institution during the bombing.

Taking stock of the situation after he had landed, Major-General R. E. Urquhart, commander of the 1st Airborne Division, was disturbed to learn that the Recce Squadron under Major C. F. H. Gough, whose initial task was to seize the Arnhem bridge by *coup de main*, had been unable to move off. The glider-borne troops and parachutists who made up the squadron were waiting for their heavily armed jeeps specially mounted with machine-guns pointing forwards and backwards, but unfortunately the gliders carrying them broke their tow ropes and never arrived. Alternative plans had to be made as, unaware of the hold-up, Brigadier Lathbury's 2nd Battalion, under Lieutenant-Colonel J. D. Frost, was racing for the bridge alone. Communications had broken down, and Urquhart, determined to find

Frost and apprise him of the situation, set off in his jeep. By then sounds of firing were heard from the direction of Arnhem.

The battalion was located east of Oosterbeek, moving slowly along the road to Arnhem, but Urquhart was told that Frost had gone on ahead after a fight with the Germans in Heveadorp in which several of his men had been lost. Elsewhere some desultory fighting had taken place and German prisoners had been captured, but soon strong German reaction was becoming evident. Mortar bombs whined over the trees and exploded with a dull, deadly plop around the cross-roads where men of the 3rd Parachute Battalion crouched down under any cover they could find. Medical orderlies had their work cut out as casualties began to mount steadily.

Field-Marshal Model, commander of German Army Group B, had missed capture by minutes as paratroops closed in on his H.Q. at the Hartenstein and Taffelberg Hotels in Oosterbeek, and he headed for the H.Q. of S.S. General Willi Bittrich's Panzer Corps in Arnhem. By an amazing piece of luck, Bittrich had been apprised of the orders for the entire Airborne Corps operations by General Student, into whose hands they had fallen after they had been recovered from the body of an American soldier killed in a glider near Vught. Bittrich made his plans accordingly, in the light of this gratuitous information and his own conception of what the British methods of operation were likely to be.

Meanwhile, Frost and his 2nd Battalion, on the move again, having disposed of the obstacles which had been slowing their progress, were breaking into Arnhem. C Company, sent to snatch the railway bridge across the Neder Rhine west of their main objective, the main road bridge, arrived just as the Germans blew it up. Undaunted, C Company dashed off to capture the German H.Q. in Arnhem. Frost, with A Company and his H.Q., raced on through the town, and as it was growing dark they came up to their objective, the bridge at Arnhem, looming above them in the half-light. The men held their breath as they watched German transport crossing to the south side. The paratroopers moved quickly to take up positions on the northern river-bank along the Ryn-Kade, below the bridge, and in houses and warehouses around the northern ramp.

From the top of a tall building at the end of Markt Straat, Frost was able to peer across the length of the bridge to the southern end where groups of S.S. men were taking up positions. Some of Frost's men were occupying a school on the west side of the approach to the bridge, while others, under Major Digby Tatham-Warter, had taken up positions almost under the massive supports of the bridge. By now Gough had managed to link up with Frost, and he occupied a tall waterworks building with a flat roof on Nieuwe Kade, about fifty yards from the bridge and with a good view along its length. A few other units, including some engineers, had moved up and were spread out in houses around the perimeter.

From under the bridge, a small party of men led by Lieutenant

Maj.-Gen. Urquhart outside his Hartenstein Hotel H.Q.

McDermont tried to make a swift rush across the bridge to the southern end, but came under relentless fire from a pill-box and a German armoured car blocking the roadway and were driven back. Another attempt was made and Lieutenant Jack Grayburn was wounded. The pill-box continued to dominate the road.

B Company, which had been sent earlier to the north of the town to deal with Germans commanding the ridge at Den Brink, were ordered to come down and make an assault on the south side of the bridge using boats found clustered around the end of a dismantled pontoon bridge. But it was not until three o'clock in the morning that the men were able to pass through the town down to the river-bank.

Meanwhile, positions around the northern approach to the bridge were consolidated. Machine-gun posts were set up and a few mines laid in readiness for a possible night counter-attack by the Germans. On the bridge, above the supports, what seemed to be a line of wooden huts could be seen, at the back of which was a pill-box. Two British sappers with a flame-thrower sneaked forward to knock out the pill-box. A spurt of flame curved around the huts and they exploded in a gigantic sheet of flame and a deafening roar. Soldiers crouched low as the blast shook the buildings and debris rained down. A shudder like an earthquake tremor ran through the ground. The huts had been chock-a-block with ammunition. Part of the bridge seemed to be on

fire, and by the eerie light of the flickering flames British and Germans peered uneasily across the bridge at each other. Later in the evening C Company of the 3rd Parachute Battalion, under Major Lewis, moved cautiously through the deserted streets of Arnhem past the railway station and along narrow shopping thoroughfares, alert for sudden German attacks. As the men came into a street leading to the bridge they ran into some Germans but had no difficulty in brushing them aside and joining Frost.

As Frost and his men steeled themselves for the German counter-attacks which they knew could be launched at any minute, word was received from the brigade commander that the rest of the 1st Brigade would not attempt to reach the bridge until the morning.

The 1st Parachute Battalion, commanded by Lieutenant-Colonel D. Dobie, ran into German armour and suffered casualties. Moving through woods around midnight, the men entered Arnhem before dawn. Harassed by mortar fire they incurred more casualties, but, having picked up a signal from Frost urgently calling for reinforce-ments, Dobie decided to turn from his fixed objective, which was the high ground north of the town, and join Frost at the bridge. Heavy opposition from enemy forces dug in around a railway bridge was encountered in the suburb of Mariendaal, and around Arnhem airborne forces were held up as more and more Germans arrived on the scene with tanks and self-propelled guns.

On Sunday evening the Hartenstein Hotel in Oosterbeek had been occupied by the British. Large groups of airborne troops were still

A glider is towed into the
air.

cluttering the side roads approaching the western side of Arnhem
at first light next morning and were cheered by Dutch civilians who
plied them with food and drink. This holiday atmosphere caused
the loss of precious minutes needed to break through to the bridge,
reinforce the garrison, and consolidate the positions for the dropping
of Brigadier Hackett's 4th Parachute Brigade later in the morning.
German troops were closing in to contain the airborne forces and
then squeeze them until their positions became untenable.

Early Monday morning, Frost and his men positioned around the
bridge saw three trucks packed with Germans approaching, running
into a perfect ambush. Only two Germans, both badly wounded,
escaped. South of the bridge a German armoured convoy started to
move forward to run the gauntlet. The parachutists waited calmly.
The convoy was allowed to reach the northern end of the bridge,
but as the leading vehicles were trundling over the approach road,
the paratroopers opened up with six-pounders, Piats, and machine-
guns. Vehicles veered aside, some swerving and toppling over the
embankment. Others caught fire. Most of the remaining vehicles
halted, unable to proceed, but a few managed to break loose only
to be knocked out before they could get far. Destruction of the convoy
was complete, and after that, although the Germans made several
attempts to launch infantry attacks across the river, mortar fire from
Frost's men, and artillery fire called up from airborne gunners positioned at Oosterbeek and directed from a forward command post
by Major Dennis Mumford, always sent them scurrying for cover.

But the Germans had no intention of leaving Frost sitting astride
his prize. They opened up a murderous mortar and artillery bombardment which caused severe casualties among the paratroopers. The

parachutists fought back fiercely, and as the Germans were man-handling a medium gun into position to bear down on the northern end of the bridge, accurate fire from the parachutists laid low the gun crew although they were unable to stop a German Mark IV tank sent to recover the gun.

Frost's men were more than holding their own, but were without any information about what their comrades elsewhere were doing or how far away the nearest unit was. They could make out that fighting was taking place somewhere to the west, but they had no idea if any progress was being made to come to their aid. Under cover of diversionary parties, Frost managed to contact Dobie with an urgent appeal for help, but by then patrols of German armour and self-propelled guns had almost sealed off the area.

Later in the afternoon, Germans moving down the east bank of the river to penetrate Frost's perimeter were met with fixed bayonets wielded by parachutists yelling their extraordinary battle-cry, "Whoa, Mohammed!" and in the fierce hand-to-hand fighting from house to house a number of British were killed and wounded. But the Germans were thrown back. Some of the German prisoners taken in this and subsequent similar actions were identified as belonging to the crack 9th and 10th S.S. Panzer Divisions. The fact that crack troops were being used against him was bad news for Frost.

As night fell, German mortars, self-propelled guns, 20mm and 40mm guns relentlessly bombarded the houses clustered around the northern end of the bridge, blasting buildings into piles of rubble and causing fires which spread rapidly, fanned by a lively breeze.

83

Maj.-Gen. Ridgway,
commander of the
American 18th Airborne
Corps.

In a nightmare of crackling flames, falling masonry, acrid smoke, and showers of spiteful sparks, the singed and scorched defenders were forced out into streets full of dancing shadows, to come under vicious sniper fire as they rushed pell-mell towards other buildings, seeking cover. The wounded were dragged off the streets by their comrades or died hidden in the shadows.

In rooms full of choking dust and stinking of cordite fumes and refuse, paratroopers waited for the Germans to come, and come they did after dosing the bridgehead again and again with incendiaries. But once more. in the bitter house-to-house fighting that followed, the enemy was hurled back into the darkness.

Frost managed to contact Divisional H.Q. with an urgent request for aid and was told that two battalions were poised to make the breakthrough during the night to bring up supplies. For the first time Frost learned that the second airlift, expected at ten in the morning, had arrived at two that afternoon. The hard-pressed paratroops were certain that the spearhead XXX Corps of the Second Army pushing up from the south was not far away, but they were wrong. Having linked up with the 101st Airborne Division at Eindhoven, the corps was bogged down at Zon. Jim Gavin's 82nd Airborne Division had captured an important ridge of high ground near Nijmegen but for the time being was prevented from taking the bridge by "Boy" Browning, who thought it more important that the Americans should hold the ridge. Fighting with grim determination to hang on to their bridgehead, Frost and his men knew nothing of the delays to the south.

The second airlift, arriving some four hours late, had a rougher reception than the first, but the planes kept coming in for an hour. Aircraft and gliders were hit by flak, and paratroopers had to leap for their lives from blazing planes. Gliders scored deep furrows as they careered along the ground and into trees, ripping off their wings and sending men somersaulting through the air like rag dolls. Fires were started on the heaths and smoke drifted across fields and meadows. Parachutists, blown off course, landed in isolated groups. The Germans pressed close around the perimeter, which was defended by men of the 7th King's Own Scottish Borderers. Yet, despite the appearance of complete chaos, the drop was successful.

But trouble was piling up for the airborne forces. As the 11th Parachute Battalion moved off to support the drive to reach Frost at the bridge, ominous reports arrived of masses of German tanks advancing down the roads from the north towards Arnhem. This confirmed earlier reports that a Panzer corps had been refitting in the area at the time of the attack. By the evening the 11th Battalion, and two companies of the 2nd Battalion, South Staffords, which had accompanied them on the march from the dropping zone, entered the western outskirts of Arnhem not far from where Urquhart had been trapped with a few officers and men in a group of houses.

Meanwhile, at the Hartenstein Hotel, Brigadier P. H. W. Hicks,

Gen. Maxwell Taylor, commander of the 101st Airborne Division.

commanding the 1st Airlanding Brigade, and Brigadier J. W. Hackett, commanding the 4th Parachute Brigade, were arguing about who was in command of the whole operation now that Urquhart was missing and what should be done about the situation at the bridge. Unfortunately Urquhart had left the situation regarding succession in the chain of command a little confused. Brigadier Lathbury, commander of the 1st Parachute Brigade, who was Urquhart's first choice to succeed him, was trapped with him and had been wounded. Hicks was his second choice, but Hackett was next in seniority. It was a fine time to be arguing the toss, with the situation so tense and fluid and Frost and his men sweating it out at the bridge.

Men of the South Staffords and some parachutists of the 11th Battalion linked up with Urquhart, releasing him from his predicament. He was told that his H.Q. had been established at the Hartenstein Hotel in Oosterbeek, so he set off in a jeep with Captain Taylor, leaving Captain Cleminson to try to rejoin the 3rd Battalion. When Urquhart finally arrived at his H.Q. he learned that Hicks was out inspecting his own brigade. When Hicks returned he and Urquhart agreed that it might have been better had Urquhart remained near the St. Elizabeth Hospital where he had been rescued, in order to co-ordinate the advance of the 1st and 3rd Battalions and the 11th Battalion and the Staffords.

A third air drop was expected, and unless the dropping zone was changed, the Poles who made up the bulk of the new drop would be in for a hot reception from the Germans. Messages sent back to that effect failed to get through. During the morning more German tanks arrived in Arnhem, and British troops trying to reach the bridge were finding themselves in serious trouble.

Meanwhile the spearhead of the Guards Armoured Division of XXX Corps had crossed the newly erected bridge at Zon, and advancing south of Nijmegen they found the American 82nd Airborne Division engaged in furious fighting with Germans pressing from the Reichwald Forest, and suffering heavy losses. The Zon bridge, defended by strong German forces, withstood attack after attack by the crack American parachutists and the Guards' tanks, many of which were knocked out.

Hackett, tied down north of Oosterbeek fighting off German thrusts which threatened to split his forces, and Hicks' Airlanding Brigade in the west and north-west also under severe attack, were ordered to disengage and move towards Arnhem in an arc south of the railway.

Brisk battles were being fought all over Arnhem as various units tried to bludgeon their way through to the bridge, and casualties continued to take a toll of the already sadly depleted forces. A few troops, disorientated and unsure of what was happening, were in a state of near panic, and it was necessary to cajole and threaten them in order to force them back to their positions. Jittery men opened fire indiscriminately, endangering their own men and wasting precious ammunition, until brought under control by more experienced officers and men.

85

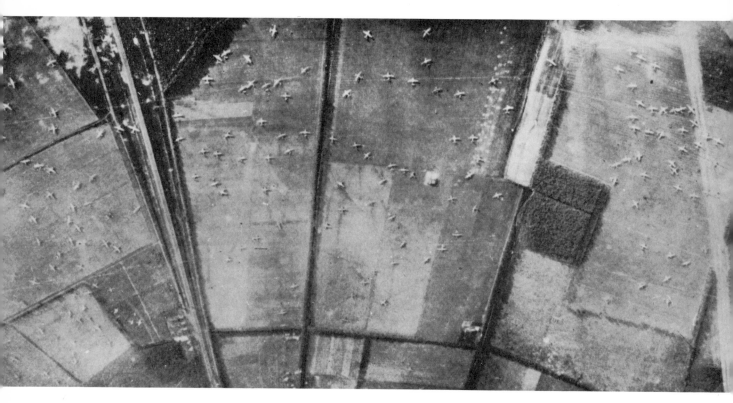

Landing zones were jammed
with gliders.

The R.A.F., not having received the signals requesting new dropping
zones for supplies, flew through heavy flak to drop their precious
loads on points now in the hands of the enemy. In vain British
troops waved scarves, staked out parachutes, and set off coloured
smoke signals to draw the attention of the aircrews to what was
happening. Supply cannisters continued to rain down on the Germans
like manna from heaven.

A Dakota, one wing ablaze, ignored the flak to come in low and
drop supplies, then turned and made a second approach to drop
the rest of its load. The pilot was Flight Lieutenant David Lord
of 271 Squadron, who had ordered his crew to bale out as he came
in to finish his job. The plane crashed in flames and Lord died.
He was awarded a posthumous Victoria Cross. Some 370 tons of
supplies and ammunition fell into the hands of the grateful Germans.
It was a bitter pill for the battered British to swallow as they watched
helpless and heartbroken through the haze of battle smoke.

Withdrawing to the Wolfhezen crossing north-west of Oosterbeek,
the 10th Battalion came under devastating fire and their casualties
were considerable. As they pushed on doggedly, the Poles began
arriving over the glider landing zone between the 10th Battalion
and the Germans. They were met with a storm of flak, and as they
landed a relentless hail of mortar bombs and machine-gun fire
fell all around them. Pressed closely by the Germans, the withdrawing 10th Battalion now found themselves under fire from the
Poles. The Poles, dressed in different uniforms from the British and
wearing grey berets, were taken for the enemy by the 10th and were

86

Troops of the 1st Light
Regiment R.A. unloading
gliders.

fired on. Not unnaturally, in the utter confusion prevailing, the Poles thought everyone in the vicinity was the enemy. They even opened fire on a company of King's Own Scottish Borderers sent to help unload their gliders.

Hackett's brigade was pounded by determined S.S. pursuers, but the airborne rearguards gave as good as they got. Captain L. Queripal of the 10th Battalion showed outstanding courage and tenacity in the retirement when, although badly wounded, he and a small group inflicted heavy losses on the enemy. He then covered the retreat of the few survivors, who last saw him hurling grenades at the enemy from a ditch. He was awarded a posthumous V.C.

By the time the 10th Battalion arrived at the railway crossing, their strength had been reduced to 250 officers and men. The 156th Battalion was not much better off, with 270 officers and men. Still the Germans did not let up. Their tanks and self-propelled guns moved up shelling the new positions taken up by the parachutists. In Arnhem itself, what was left of the 1st and 3rd Battalions of the 1st Parachute Brigade was also under heavy pressure. The South Staffords had managed to capture a building called the Monastery and win a brief respite, but on their right flank, closer to the river, the Germans were making

good use of tanks and self-propelled guns to punish the remnants of the 1st and 3rd Battalions who, although without anti-tank guns, were working miracles with their Piats. As the parachutists pushed slowly on toward the bridge, their ranks thinned as men were killed and the wounded were left in houses along the way.

By now retreat from the perimeter was beginning to become disorderly. Hungry, battle-weary stragglers, short of ammunition, drew in towards Oosterbeek as German tanks rumbled along the roads around Arnhem with impunity. On the western outskirts of the town the situation was even more chaotic. Without liaison between one group of parachutists and another there could be no co-ordination of action, and fighting was confused. Gradually as troops became even more disorganized many fell back on Oosterbeek itself, wandering around adding to the confusion. Efforts were made to reorganize the despondent men for another movement towards the bridge. Casualties had been mounting alarmingly, and Colonel Graeme Warrack, the chief doctor, worked like a Trojan as his Red Cross jeeps rushed around the area picking up wounded and taking them to makeshift hospitals and dressing stations.

Amazingly, despite the confusion in and around Arnhem, the Dutch public telephone service was still operating, and Warrack was able to call the St. Elizabeth Hospital and speak to a surprised medical officer, Captain Derek Ridler, who told Warrack that he and his staff had over eighty wounded under their care, but were coping well enough although fighting was taking place all around the hospital.

Nearer the river, the Germans tried to grind through positions held by a mixed force under Major D. Lonsdale. As three German tanks nosed out of a wood they came on Sergeant Baskerfield of the South Staffords manning an anti-tank gun sited at a crossroads. With his first shot the sergeant knocked out the leading tank and then disabled a second. German infantry crowding around the third tank started to make a dash across the road but were brought up sharply by rifle fire. But Baskerfield's gun was destroyed and as he tried to get another gun, whose crew had been killed, into action, he himself was killed. For his bravery Baskerfield won a posthumous V.C.

It was growing dark and rain was falling as survivors of the 3rd Battalion were pulled back to join remnants of other units at Oosterbeek church. The men gathered inside the small building, sprawling wearily on the stone-flagged floor or stretching out on the pews. Both hands swathed in bandages, Lonsdale rallied his mixed force with a blunt speech.

Soon the men were outside preparing defensive positions to meet the expected German onslaught. Among their number there were even a few glider pilots who, as well as being pilots, were also highly trained infantrymen, and they took up positions under Major Robert Cain of the South Staffords. The rumble of German guns and the spiteful chattering of Spandaus was drawing closer. The men were silent. They waited and they sweated.

At the bridge Frost and his men had managed to snatch a little fitful sleep, but they were in sore need of food and ammunition. It was almost impossible for the paratroopers to move between the houses they were occupying, as the Germans shot at everything that moved. From Oosterbeek, Lieutenant-Colonel "Sheriff" Thompson's gunners made it uncomfortable for Germans trying to bring 20mm and 40mm anti-aircraft guns to bear on Frost's machine-guns, but this did little to relieve the almost unbearable pressure on the defiant 2nd Battalion. Hopefully the men waited for relief.

German tanks edged forward trying to bulldoze the buildings occupied by paratroopers. Some houses were set on fire as, tenaciously, the defenders clung to their pounded positions. Piles of rubble

The German opposition:
Left to right, Field-
Marshal Model, General
Student, General Bittrich,
Major Kraust, and General
Harmenl.

Troops of the German 1st
Parachute Army.

blocked the streets and choking red brick-dust rose above the inferno. The stifling conditions for the men in the houses were bad enough, but the plight of the wounded was beyond all endurance. There was no possibility of evacuating them, and they were packed in the cavernous cellars below the H.Q. building together with more than 150 German prisoners. There were only two medical officers and a few orderlies to take care of the wounded.

Every now and then hand-to-hand fighting would break out as squads of Germans tried to infiltrate the British positions. Parties of parachutists ventured forth with Piats and grenades to stalk German tanks, and nowhere did the Germans manage to crack wide the British defences. Frost and Gough discussed the idea of a swift sortie across the bridge to try and link up with XXX Corps, but Frost decided this would be suicidal and that it would be better not to squander any of his dwindling forces. To the embattled men of the 2nd Battalion and their comrades of C Company of the 3rd Battalion it seemed that Arnhem was collapsing in flames about their ears.

The shrinking 1st Airborne Brigade was deployed around Oosterbeek, and the men knew that unless XXX Corps arrived on the scene soon they faced the grim prospect of a battle of attrition – one they could not win.

It was drizzling as Wednesday, September 20, dawned to the accompaniment of a heavy German mortar bombardment which shook the divisional area in Oosterbeek. Hackett, who had not yet drawn in his brigade to the divisional area, was hotly engaged by Germans on both flanks and to his front. Moreover, German tanks had broken into his positions and were marauding at will, threatening to scatter his forces.

It soon became apparent that as a cohesive force the 1st Parachute Brigade had ceased to exist. All that remained was the 2nd Battalion and a company of the 3rd Battalion fighting at the bridge. The South Staffords had been fragmented and the 11th Parachute Battalion had disintegrated. Although he did not know it, Frost at the bridge was on his own.

The Germans were astride every road into Arnhem, and Tiger tanks against which the paratroopers had no defence had made their terrifying appearance around the perimeter. The idea of a breakthrough by paratroopers from Oosterbeek to the bridge at Arnhem was no longer feasible. Urquhart ordered Hackett to bring the remains of his brigade into position on the north side of the Oosterbeek area. Gough managed to phone Urquhart from the bridge, and it was with heavy heart that Urquhart had to give the cheerful Recce major to understand that only the arrival of XXX Corps could save what was left of the 1st Airborne Brigade from their present terrible predicament. During the morning the Germans intensified their bombardment of the whole battle zone. The hotel was hit several times, and debris strewed the lawns, where unburied corpses lay grotesquely beside smashed vehicles, weapons, and boughs sheered from trees by flying chunks of metal. Crouched in their weapon pits dug beneath trees and bushes in the hotel grounds, men with red-rimmed eyes and anxious, grubby faces waited uncertainly for whatever new horror the day might bring. Beyond the H.Q., groups of men from many broken units fought on with dogged courage and determination.

At the bloody Arnhem bridge the paratroopers were under continuous attack. Enemy tanks pressed close and lashed furiously at the groggy British troops in the shattered houses. The area surrounding the bridge approach was a shambles and only the bridge itself was still intact, but the men of the 2nd Battalion and their comrades of the 3rd Battalion continued to resist all efforts to shake them loose from their positions.

Hackett, trying to extricate his 4th Brigade, was in serious trouble, and Wilson's Independent Company and the 1st Battalion, Border Regiment, came under attack from strong German forces. The divisional area was under intermittent bombardment by mortars and artillery, and still there was no sign of XXX Corps. Unfortunately the Allied Tactical Air Force was not committed to support the Airborne enclave. Rocket attacks by Allied planes on German troops, guns, and armour around the Oosterbeek perimeter could have done much to mitigate the agony of the paratroopers, who were suffering heavy shelling to which they had no effective reply.

Conditions in the Hartenstein Hotel had deteriorated to a revolting degree. Dirty, unshaven officers and men packed the cellars, almost suffocating in the stench and fug. There were no latrines, and it was foolhardy to use the grounds swept by mortar blasts and shellfire.

Hackett's 4th Brigade was still taking tremendous punishment from all sides as it tried to reach the divisional area. Short of ammunition and with some weapons rendered useless by hard wear, the paratroopers resorted to using captured German material. The 10th Battalion was now leading the withdrawal, while the 156th Battalion was fighting a rearguard action, but movement was slow. The men had to fight every inch of the way, and when what was left of the battalion, just sixty officers and men, limped into the H.Q. area, they were filthy and exhausted. Yet they were not at the end of their tether. They took up positions in several houses which commanded the crossroads to wait for the enemy, and many of the men who had survived the nightmare march died there.

Meanwhile Hackett and the rest of his men were being cut to pieces. The German's tried every trick to grind them into the dust, but they fought on. Hackett rallied the hundred-odd survivors in a hollow and there they resisted all German attempts to dislodge them. Led by Hackett himself, a squad of parachutists made a desperate sortie to silence a troublesome German machine-gun. Then German tanks came thundering up, and as casualties mounted fast Hackett decided that his only chance was to break through the German ring with fixed bayonets.

Yelling their battle-cry, the parachutists charged and cut through

This German poster
glorified Nazi youth.

An American poster
warning against careless
talk.

the Germans. They kept going, and in a little while were amazed and delighted to reach the comparative safety of strong positions held by the Border Regiment on the west side of the perimeter. Hackett arrived with seventy officers and men to take up positions south of the 10th Battalion.

Urquhart's main concern now was to hold the perimeter on the north bank, retaining the divisional area at Oosterbeek as a bridgehead until the arrival of the Second Army. There was no hope of reaching the Arnhem bridge, but there was heartening news that the Guards Armoured Division was in the vicinity of Nijmegen and was pushing on. Seventy Dakotas came flying in low to drop supplies, but once again, despite urgent messages and all manner of ground signals, the supplies were dropped in the German lines.

A battle developed around the dressing station at the Hotel Schoonhord, and the building was struck by shells while the wounded were being evacuated. Before long the Germans had overrun the hospital, and walking wounded who were still arriving for treatment were taken prisoner. Despite its capture, the hospital was still under fire from German snipers, and the German soldier left to guard the dressing station was not at all happy about his situation.

Word got around that patrols of the Second Army had been sighted

The bridge, with remnants of a German column on the northern approach.

across the river, and for a while this perked up the tired paratroopers around the perimeter. But still they were hammered by mortar bombs and shells, and still the Germans were moving inexorably towards their cramped positions.

At the bridge, the indomitable Frost, nicknamed "the mad Colonel" by the Germans, had been badly wounded in the leg and Gough had taken over command, although he deferred to Frost on major decisions. The unflagging Tatham-Warter took over the remains of the 2nd Battalion. When the Germans set houses ablaze, forcing paratroopers into the open, Lieutenant Grayburn led patrols to keep probing German groups "on the hop". Dispersed paratroopers reformed and regained some of their old positions. Grayburn with his patrols created a diversion while British sappers defused demolition charges which the Germans had fixed in various places under the bridge. Grayburn was wounded in one of the sorties and later killed. He was awarded a posthumous V.C. for his sustained courage and bravery.

At dusk, three bren-gun carriers packed with food and ammunition moved out of the divisional area in an attempt to break through to Frost under cover of darkness. They never made it. One was hit by a shell almost immediately and blew up, another was forced to turn back, and the third just disappeared into the night and was never seen again. Meanwhile, in the basement of a big warehouse near the bridge, over two hundred wounded, many seriously injured, were packed together in wretched conditions. The two medical officers and a few orderlies were hard put to it to give them any measure

94

A view of the bridge from the southern end, held by the Germans.

of attention as the fighting raged outside. The Germans started using phosphorus shells and soon the building caught fire. The doctors informed Gough that unless the .wounded were surrendered without delay they would be roasted alive. Under cover of the Red Cross flag two of the orderlies came out of the building and managed to make an arrangement with the Germans for the evacuation of the wounded. The Germans agreed that both sides should hold their fire while the work of evacuation was going on, but they took advantage of the situation to infiltrate the British positions which were still being held, and they commandeered the few remaining British jeeps, ostensibly to remove the wounded.

Soon the fight was raging again as fiercely as before. The British situation had become hopeless as food and water ran out and little ammunition remained. A few paratroopers tried to make a break for the divisional sector, but were cut down before they could get very far. The Germans were ready to make a concerted effort to wipe out the few remaining paratroopers clustered around the devastated northern approaches to the bridge.

In the dull light of a cheerless dawn, entrenched in cellars and behind mounds of rubble close to similar British positions across the streets, the Germans intensified their fire and they did not lack ammunition. Worn to the bone the British paratroopers fought to their last round, then one by one they were winkled out. German

95

The Hartenstein Hotel at
Oosterbeek.

A British six-pounder fires
from a shop window.

A six-pounder in action
against a German self-
propelled gun eighty yards
away.

infantry picked their way through piles of debris, tossing grenades into cellars, through shattered windows and doorways, wherever they thought paratroopers were hiding. Survivors, including Gough, were waiting to make their escape. And then it was all over. The Germans had secured their bridge although at a frightful cost. Their dead littered the bridge and the surrounding area. Burned-out vehicles were cleared from the roadways and soon German armour was moving south across the bridge unchecked. The British plan had been to hold the bridge for twenty-four hours until XXX Corps arrived to consolidate the bridgehead and roll the Germans back into Germany. Frost and his men had held their positions for three days and four nights against some of Germany's best troops. But all in vain. Horrocks was still miles away to the south when the 2nd Battalion had finally shot its bolt, but the agony for the rest of the 1st Airborne Division was not yet over.

Around Oosterbeek, Urquhart divided his forces into two commands. The western section, under Hicks, consisted of the survivors of three companies of the Border Regiment, some men of the King's Own Scottish Borderers, the Independent Company, and a collection of glider pilots, sappers, and a few Poles. The eastern section commanded by Hackett, comprised the remnants of the 10th and 156th Battalions, "Sheriff" Thompson's 1st Light Regiment, Royal Artillery, the Lonsdale Force made up of survivors from the 1st, 3rd, and 11th Parachute Battalions and South Staffords, some glider pilots, and a group of miscellaneous troops who had become separated from their battalions.

In all, some three thousand men were packed within the perimeter where practically every road was impassable to transport because of piles of rubble and debris, shattered wrecks of vehicles, felled trees, broken railings, twisted wire, and unburied dead.

97

A British six-pounder on the move towards Arnhem.

But some help for the beleaguered force was on hand. Divisional signallers had managed to make contact with the 64th Medium Regiment, Royal Artillery, eleven miles to the south with the Second Army, and soon the gunners opened up with a series of shots quickly supplemented by a battery of heavies. Directed by Loder-Symonds from an observation post within the perimeter, the gunners succeeded in breaking up several German attacks, relieving some of the pressure on the airborne troops and boosting their morale.

At Urquhart's hotel headquarters, conditions were rapidly worsening. There was trouble with the frightened German prisoners herded in the makeshift compound – the tennis courts in the hotel grounds. They complained that they were exposed to shellfire and that they had had no food. They were told that everyone was in the same boat and were given shovels and told to dig themselves in. As for food, they were told they could have twice as much as the British, which was none.

The desultory plonk-plonk of mortaring and the whining of bullets ricocheting from walls of buildings was general in the divisional area, but although the Germans continued their probing there were no concerted attacks. The mortars were taking their toll, however. Hackett was touring his new area of command with his new brigade major, Maddon, when a mortar-bomb-burst killed Maddon outright and wounded Hackett in the face and hands. "Sheriff" Thompson was hit and badly wounded in the stomach. Work in the hospitals and dressing stations never slackened.

In the afternoon the R.A.F. twice attempted to drop supplies to the besieged. The arrival of the first of the British aircraft over the dropping zone was greeted by German fighters which played havoc with the slow-moving planes. The second drop was at 1600 hours, and this time some ammunition and food were picked up by the paratroopers. In the operation the R.A.F. lost 20 per cent of the aircraft taking part. An hour later Polish parachutists arrived over their dropping zone, south of the river just east of Driel, but by then the Heveadorp ferry, which could have been used to transport the Poles across to Oosterbeek, was in German hands. Urquhart's chief engineer, Lieutenant-Colonel Eddie Myers, scoured the river, boathouses, and sheds for boats and rafts for use in the crossing and set men to work converting jeep trailers into rafts.

The Germans reacted violently to the Polish landings, attacking them in the dropping zone and disputing their every effort to organize their widely dispersed groups. The Germans also launched fierce attacks on the King's Own Scottish Borderers to the north. Once more the 64th Medium Regiment, Royal Artillery, came to the rescue and the King's Own Scottish Borderers succeeded in reoccupying their positions. But their casualties were grievous and they were forced to draw in their line, leaving themselves dangerously exposed. The Germans started attacking one after another of the British positions. First it was the turn of the Lonsdale Force. An hour later the Border Regiment came under attack, and at 0810 hours, the Germans launched a fierce onslaught on the 10th Battalion, setting ablaze the houses they were occupying and forcing them out.

Unable to cross to the north side of the river, the Poles took up defensive positions near Driel. They could do nothing to help the British cooped up in Oosterbeek, and as darkness fell the paratroopers in precarious positions around the perimeter, with the smell of death in the air, prepared to face another miserable night of cold and uncertainty.

At the Hartenstein, Urquhart decided to draw in the horseshoe-shaped perimeter and redeploy his forces. He knew that, unless relief arrived soon, he would be squeezed until no room remained for manoeuvre, and worse still, if the Germans cut him off from the river there could be no hope of withdrawal should it become necessary. Urquhart sent a message to Corps explaining the situation and the fact that his resources were stretched to the utmost.

Just before dawn on Friday, September 22, Lieutenant-Colonel Stevens, the British liaison officer with the Poles on the south side of the Neder Rhine, made a precarious crossing of the river and turned up at Urquhart's H.Q. He told the commander that XXX Corps were pressing hard, but was unable to give specific details, so Urquhart was still in the dark.

As the Germans started what had become their customary dawn bombardment and the Hartenstein rattled with thunderous explosions, Urquhart received a signal to the effect that 43 Division had been ordered to pull out all the stops to reach the Heveadorp ferry, and that if necessary Urquhart should withdraw his forces to the other side. Now, although the Germans controlled the ferry, Urquhart was prepared to recapture it. But he was far from satisfied with the speed, progress, and the efforts being made by XXX Corps, and he decided to send his chief staff officer, Lieutenant-Colonel Charles B. Mackenzie, across the river to explain in detail the desperate situation at Oosterbeek and the need for the utmost urgency on the part of XXX Corps. The Germans were already back at work making probing attacks around the perimeter, and mortaring was heavy.

Urquhart told Mackenzie that he should leave XXX Corps in no doubt as to the urgent need for men, food, ammunition, and medical supplies, as well as D.U.K.W.s to ferry the Poles across to Oosterbeek. With Mackenzie went Eddie Myers, who knew most about the possibilities and hazards of using the ferry.

The two men made the perilous crossing and reached the Poles, who had been joined by a troop of British armoured cars of the Household Cavalry which had made a daring dash ahead of XXX Corps from Oosterhuit. Mackenzie signalled Urquhart's message to Horrocks, who replied that everything was being done to get essentials through.

Urquhart's bitter disappointment at the slow progress of XXX Corps was reflected in his understandable criticism of the attack in Oosterhuit by a battalion of 43 Division, which had resulted in the capture of only 139 prisoners, an obsolete tank, and six guns, at a cost of just nineteen wounded. In contrast, within the perimeter, men were dying by the dozen, and hundreds of wounded men lying on stretchers or on the floors in shattered buildings and cellars were being wounded again or blasted into eternity by German SP guns and mortars.

The perimeter defences were also under continuous bombardment by SP guns, and more houses where paratroopers sought cover were set ablaze. In the drizzling rain low grey clouds hung over Oosterbeek like dirty, dripping Army blankets. Parachutists, their faces caked with dust and streaked with smuts, beat off every attack by German infantry, but there was no defence against the Tiger tanks and SP guns ranging boldly far and wide in the knowledge that there was little to fear from the light British weapons. Nevertheless, using Piats with skill and daring, the paratroopers succeeded in knocking out some German armour.

Major Robert Cain of the South Staffords kept the German armour at bay for a time with an anti-tank gun and a section of men, and when the anti-tank gun was no longer serviceable used a Piat. German infantry trying to approach under cover of an SP gun were soon seen off by Cain's section.

Not far away, the house near Oosterbeek church being used as a hospital was crammed to suffocation with British wounded. There was little room for the hard-worked orderlies to move around to attend to their patients. Water was in short supply, and along the shell-swept path to a waterpump in a garden some fifty yards away sprawled the bodies of dead paratroopers. The house was struck repeatedly by fragments of flying metal from mortar bombs and shells and was always a target for German snipers.

South of the river some British tanks, bren-carriers, and infantry and a few D.U.K.W.s had managed to reach the Polish positions, but not before several British tanks had been put out of action by Polish mines. The plan was to put the Poles across the river that night. Two companies of the Duke of Cornwall's Light Infantry moved up to cover the crossing, but the D.U.K.W.s to be used to ferry troops bogged down on the steep muddy banks. Just before midnight a few Poles succeeded in crossing the river despite swift currents which swept many men away to be drowned or thrown up on the banks into the arms of the Germans. The presence of a few Poles in the divisional area could hardly ease the situation, which was growing more chaotic by the minute.

As Saturday morning, September 23, dawned, damp, smoke-laden mist shrouded the battle area, and drizzling rain soaked the men pitifully curled up in their weapon pits. Soon the SP guns and mortars were busy again, pounding the parachutists as they tried to freshen up a little by wiping their begrimed faces and red-rimmed eyes with rain-soaked scarves and handkerchiefs, or squatted uncomfortably exposed to answer calls of nature. Those who were lucky enough to have water and a little tea brewed up, in muddy slit trenches covered by ground-sheets, but most of the men within the perimeter had been without rations for twenty-four hours.

High explosives blasted buildings, and incendiaries started fresh fires among already burnt out and still smouldering ruins. Men darting from blazing houses amid tumbling rafters, falling masonry, and showers of hot sparks came under fire from infiltrated German snipers and had to run the gauntlet of whizzing mortar bomb fragments to reach a place of comparative safety.

Meanwhile after a hair-raising journey Mackenzie got through to XXX Corps and General Browning's H.Q., but Horrocks and Browning were having problems of their own with Germans pressing on their flanks, cutting the Second Army corridor between Veghel and Uden, and the situation there had to be restored before the drive on Arnhem could be continued. All the same, Mackenzie had the horrible feeling that nobody wanted to face up to the fact that the 1st Airborne Division trapped within the perimeter, now nick-named the Cauldron, was facing annihilation unless the Second Army was galvanized into swift and incisive action. As Mackenzie returned to the Neder Rhine in the company of the leading brigade of 43 Division, he had serious misgivings about the Polish Brigade being put under the command of the brigade of 43 Division for the proposed night crossing of the river. He thought that the independent-minded Polish Major-General Sosabowski would bitterly resent being subordinate to a comparatively junior commander. Mackenzie was

right about that, and he did everything he could to smooth the ruffled feathers of the fiery Pole.

On Saturday afternoon in the face of heavy flak 120 unescorted Stirlings and Dakotas attempted to drop supplies in the Cauldron, but as usual most of the panniers went adrift and once more the Germans were the recipients of free gifts. Sixty-three aircraft were damaged and six were lost. This was the last of the futile attempts made from England to supply the troops at Arnhem.

Urquhart felt impelled to prepare a signal to XXX Corps making absolutely clear the dire circumstances of his gallant band of heroes. The signal, dispatched at 2025 hours, stated:

> Many attacks during the day by small parties of SP guns and tanks including flamethrowers. Each attack accompanied by heavy mortaring and shelling within Divisional perimeter. After many alarms and excursions the latter remains substantially unchanged, although very thinly held. Physical contact not yet made with those on south bank of river. Resupply a flop, small quantities of ammunition gathered in. Still no food and all ranks extremely dirty owing to shortage of water. Morale still adequate, but continual heavy mortaring and shelling is having obvious effects. We shall hold out but at the same time hope for a brighter 24 hours ahead.

The message was a restrained appraisal of the terrible situation in the perimeter by a cool, brave, and dignified commander whose men were giving everything they had to maintain a precarious toehold on the north side of the Neder Rhine and had a right to expect extreme efforts and sacrifice to be made on their behalf.

Brig. "Pip" Hicks.

Brig. Hackett.

Brig. Gerald Lathbury.

103

By nightfall the rain had stopped and stars peeped out over the dismal ruins of the Cauldron. Dancing flames from the blazing gasworks in the south-west corner of the perimeter were reflected in the river. Intermittent bursts of fire from the SP guns ripped open the shadows to reveal the stark scene, where tired, hungry, dirty men cowered in their holes waiting for, praying for, the long-overdue relief. The perimeter had shrunk still further as it soaked up German attacks, but the line held.

Mackenzie, returning from his mission, was ferried back across the river and reached the Hartenstein just before midnight, and he told Urquhart what plans had been made for the night crossing of the river by the Poles and the British infantry. Urquhart had to be satisfied with that, although he could hardly be expected to be too sanguine about the enterprise's overall benefit to his forces.

Indeed, the brigade of 43 Division had no more than twelve boats with which to ferry the men across the river, and by early Sunday morning only two hundred Polish parachutists had reached the north side, where they were deployed to reinforce Hackett's positions.

At the Hartenstein H.Q., the windows had been barricaded with furniture, and men were posted ready to fight off any direct German attack, while in the dank, reeking cellars signalmen bent over radio sets trying to raise the Second Army for news of its progress. Mortar bombs burst in and around the hotel grounds, where bodies of the dead still lay unburied and German snipers were shooting at anything that moved in the vicinity. While trying to organize his Polish reinforcements Hackett was wounded in the thigh and stomach by a mortar burst. The chief doctor, Colonel Warrack, was at the Hartenstein at the time, and he attended to his wounds. The general situation of the wounded at the Hartenstein was so bad that Warrack was convinced that the time had come to evacuate all the wounded within the perimeter to hospitals in Arnhem, and he obtained permission from Urquhart to try to arrange the evacuation with the Germans. He was, however, warned that on no account was he to prejudice the continued resistance of the parachutists.

Accompanied by a Dutch doctor and by Lieutenant-Commander Wolters, Warrack made contact with the German medical officer at the Hotel Schoonhord, and from there they were taken to the German H.Q. in Arnhem. The Germans agreed to evacuate the British wounded and ordered a convoy of ambulances to be prepared for that purpose. Warrack then returned to the divisional area and proceeded to organize the evacuation. Two hundred walking wounded moved off first, and in an uneasy truce, broken by sporadic firing and an occasional flare-up, a further 250 men, including the redoubtable Hackett, were moved by ambulance and jeep to hospitals in Arnhem, where they received attention by teams of British, German, and Dutch medical staff.

Then the battle went on unabated, the Germans increasing their mortaring and shelling and becoming more persistent in their infantry

A Sherman of the Guards Armoured Division passing a knocked-out German tank on the road to Arnhem.

attacks. But still the defenders of the perimeter managed to hurl them back and even made sorties to throw them off balance.

Urquhart managed to establish radio contact with Major-General Thomas, commander of 43 Division across the river, and told him of the desperate plight of the 1st Airborne Division. But Thomas was brusque, and Urquhart, tried almost beyond endurance, was infuriated, especially as he was well aware that the side of the river from which Thomas offered gratuitous advice was a paradise compared to the Cauldron. Also, support from Allied fighters and bombers was minimal, and plans for an emergency airdrop of supplies were strangled in red tape.

By now Horrocks, who had visited Sosabowski at Driel, decided that another attempt to cross the river should be made on Monday night, September 25. But Browning had other ideas. He thought that the time had come to cut their losses and withdraw what was left of the 1st Airborne Division to the south side of the river; and it was easy to sell the idea to General Dempsey, for Field-Marshal Model was seriously threatening the flanks of the extended XXX Corps and also holding up the advance of VIII Corps and XII Corps, preventing them from moving up on the flanks of XXX Corps.

Horrocks was still in favour of forcing a crossing of the Neder Rhine; but Dempsey and Browning had decided against it, and Montgomery assented to the withdrawal of the 1st Airborne Division. They could have had little confidence that much could be retrieved from the disaster of Arnhem. What did they consider were the chances of bringing back a shattered force of utterly exhausted and disillusioned men across the Neder Rhine? They had shown themselves incapable of pushing across more or less fresh troops to reinforce

A vehicle of the Guards Armoured Division is hit and bursts into flames on the road from Nijmegen to Arnhem.

and consolidate the Oosterbeek bridgehead which the 1st Airborne had been holding against all odds for over a week, and were still holding.

In the early hours of Monday morning the 4th Battalion, Dorsets, started across the river to help in the evacuation. The current carried away most of their boats beyond the perimeter and casualties were heavy. Eddie Myers, who had been directing the loading of the D.U.K.W.s, later made his way along the river embankment past German positions to reach the Hartenstein, carrying messages to Urquhart. One from Browning, not very helpful nor very inspiring, concluded: "It may amuse you to know that my front faces in all directions, but I am only in close contact with enemy for about eight thousand yards to the south east, which is quite enough in present circumstances."

Urquhart, understandably, was not amused.

The other message was from Thomas. Written much later, it explained that the plan to form a bridgehead west of Arnhem was being dropped, and that Urquhart and Thomas should fix a time for the withdrawal of the 1st Airborne Division to the south of the river. The operation had the curious designation Operation Berlin.

By this time the battle area was a stinking shambles. The morning had no cheer for the wet, near-starving paratroopers still holding a persistent enemy at bay. Seventy-five per cent of the formidable force which had landed with such panache just over a week before had been wiped out. Two and a half thousand battered warriors remained on their feet to deny the enemy a complete victory. Dressing stations which Warrack's deal with the Germans had practically

106

Some air drops got through:
British soldiers open
panniers.

emptied were near full again with newly wounded, and their suffering was hellish. Corpses were strewn everywhere, and the sight was demoralizing to the survivors, who, by now, had given up hope of ever coming out of the Cauldron alive.

But the decision to carry out Operation Berlin that night had been made, and at Divisional H.Q. details were being worked out to start the evacuation of the north bank of the river at 2200 hours, the men moving in groups of fourteen, each group hopefully representing a boatload. To Myers fell the task of detailing guides to shepherd the groups by selected routes to the marshy river-bank, where a ferry service had been arranged. However, as practically a whole day had still to be sweated out, Urquhart decided, wisely, not to tell the men of the evacuation plans until the last minute. He could not take the risk that a wounded man falling into German hands might leak the news. At it was, the Germans started to press harder than ever to cut the parachutists off from the river. They broke into the area where the few British batteries of 75mm guns were positioned, and were met with devastating fire over open sights.

Hospital buildings were falling to bits, swept by shell-fire and mortar blasts, and the Taffelberg Hotel had to be evacuated, the wounded being carted off on wheelbarrows, handcarts, and even makeshift sleds. Before long other dressing stations and hospitals, collapsing about the heads of the hapless wounded and the harassed staff, had to be abandoned and more men were lost in the process.

During the course of the afternoon more Germans infiltrated the perimeter, and one group with a machine-gun came out of a wood

107

Arnhem V.C. winners: Capt.
Queripal, Maj. Robert
Cain, Sgt. Baskerfield, Lt.
Grayburn and Flt. Lt. Lord.

Major Robert Cain, VC

Captain L. E. Queripel, VC

Lieutenant J. H. Grayburn, VC

Sergeant J. D. Baskerfield, VC

Flight-Lieutenant D. S. A. Lord,
VC

108

A Canadian poster to help
the war effort.

It was a job to sell cod in
World War II. This poster
was designed to help.

One of the German dead.

just a few hundred yards from the Hartenstein to take up a position covering one of the proposed escape routes. A shoot from the 64th Medium, Royal Artillery, was called up by Lieutenant-Colonel Loder-Symonds, who directed the gunners, and from a range of some fifteen thousand yards they bombarded the shocked Germans in the middle of the perimeter.

It was planned that, even as the work of evacuation was progressing, British radio operators would keep on sending messages until the last minute, with occasional gaps at irregular intervals, so as to give the Germans no inkling of what was taking place. All German prisoners were to be ordered into slit trenches, where they would no doubt be glad to stay for the night because of the now continual heavy shelling, and it was hoped that they would not realize that the British had gone until the morning. Just to make sure, a few military police volunteered to stay behind to guard them; they would try to escape later. Alan Wood, the gutsy *Daily Express* war correspondent who was with the 1st Airborne from start to finish, wrote that it was hoped that the Germans would gradually close in on the perimeter and start fighting each other before they woke up to the fact that the paratroopers were no longer in the middle.

While the fighting continued, everything that could be done to prepare for the hazardous evacuation was done. Guides familiarized themselves with the routes, parachute tapes were used to mark out guide lines, and boats were made ready at the river's edge. When everything was set, the battered survivors within the perimeter were

109

British three-inch mortar in action.

British patrol in Oosterbeek.

told. Their feelings were mixed. They had hoped for relief and that the bridgehead they had established would be taken over by XXX Corps and exploited. Had all the hardship and bloody sacrifice in the Cauldron been in vain? Did it have to end in inglorious evacuation after nine days of hell? But none of the men could feel sorry at the chance to get away from that awful perimeter where the nauseating stench of corpses cloyed in their nostrils: away from the constant threat of death or maiming, from filth and squalor and the deafening din and blinding smoke of continuous battle. The para-troopers, weak from the lack of food and water, were fighting mostly with German weapons. Most of their own had become unserviceable through constant use, or were without ammunition. There was no time to lose now. Already groups of parachutists had become isolated from each other, and communications between them were becoming increasingly difficult.

As night fell the men waited tensely for their turn to move off. They had blackened their already dirty faces with mud and had secured their accoutrements to stop them rattling and clanking. They muffled their boots by wrapping them in strips of cloth or blanket and pulling socks over them. It was a dark night with heavy rain whipped by blustery winds: a miserable night, but in some measure helpful for the perilous move down to the marsh and across the river.

Tracer shells fired by an anti-aircraft battery of 43 Division streaked over the two river routes, guiding the bedraggled parachutists to the river-bank. British artillery on the south side started a heavy bombard-ment, hammering the German positions around the perimeter while British infantry kept up a lively small-arms fire to cover the crossings.

The night was wild and dangerous. Strong currents carried away some of the boats; others stuck fast in the glutinous mud of the river-banks. Men coming down to the river could hardly raise their feet, for their blanket-swathed boots were now like great footballs of mud. But the work of evacuation went steadily on. Boats were landing men in safety and going back for more. The men groped their way along the taped escape routes, holding on to the smocks of the men in front, and were kept on course by glider pilots spaced out along the routes to keep the parachutists on the right path.

The whites of their eyes gleaming through the mud, groups of saturated paratroopers waited like zombies in the muddy meadows by the river to be picked up by the boats. Badly wounded men had begged their comrades to help them to the river, and they were placed gently in the ferry boats. But progress was nail-bitingly slow, espe-cially as half the boats were sunk in the first hour.

Mortar bombs fell among groups of men huddled in the slime. Shells were falling in Oosterbeek, drowning the noise of the storm boats' engines. Inevitably, bands of paratroopers trudging through the mud lost their bearings. One group of about fifty glider pilots joined a group of war correspondents and public relations men. They all tailed down to the river, where two assault craft were ferrying

Men of the K.O.S.B. outside
Arnhem.

German prisoners being
marched to the Hartenstein
compound.

112

back and forth, and flopped down on the wet grass to wait patiently in sopping rain for their turn to be lifted to safety.

Boats collided in mid-stream, throwing the occupants into the icy water where they threshed about until picked up. Some managed to swim to the far bank and wallow ashore. Others were carried away by the current into the night and drowned. The rain was coming down in buckets as more and more parties were ferried to the southern bank, where the sodden men scrambled over marsh and climbed slippery groynes and concrete dykes to reach firmer ground. Many men, having reached safety, joined in the efforts to help others across.

At 0130 hours the rearguard were beginning to withdraw from the perimeter in Oosterbeek. Near the church the Light Regiment, Royal Artillery, fired their last salvoes, then removed the breach blocks and sights from their guns to dump them in the river on the way out. As dawn began to streak the dreary sky the Germans saw that the area was unusually still, and with the realization of what had taken place, and indeed, was still taking place, they began to shell the river, sinking a boat.

Hundreds of paratroopers were still crowding the north bank hoping to be saved from the Germans. But now the ferry had ceased to exist. Heavy German machine-gun fire traversed the river. Many of the men were heartbroken after all they had been through, and those who could swim were not ready to submit to being taken prisoner. They plunged into the icy water and struck out for the south bank. But the current was swift and treacherous. Exhausted and weak with hunger and fatigue, some were swept away and dragged down by the weight of their clothing. Others, experienced and determined swimmers, tore off their clothes and swam naked to the southern bank.

The men left behind raged and swore into the night as German tanks began to move cautiously into Oosterbeek, firing point-blank into houses along the way. Some German infantry were within the perimeter, and there was sporadic firing as groups of British stragglers still refused to give up. But the battle for Arnhem was over.

In a commandeered jeep Warrack and teams of his medical staff searched the stricken town for wounded, and soon Germans joined in the search, using thirty-six ambulances. Over three hundred wounded were picked up. British walking wounded were marshalled together near the village hall by the Germans. Two hundred men went into hiding hoping to escape later: many were hidden by brave Dutchmen.

Nine days after the mighty air armada from Britain had dropped ten thousand men, including over a thousand glider pilots, only two thousand came out of the Cauldron with their gallant leader on that ghastly night of September 25–26, 1944. Twelve hundred officers and men had died at Arnhem.

Trailers for television

DURING WORLD WAR II I DID MOST OF MY CINEMAGOING AT "flea pits" in small towns and villages, garrison cinemas, and army camps, but I liked the films none the less for that provided they were tolerable or I was in a tolerant mood. I could not have been in a tolerant mood when I went to see *Rebecca* in 1940, for I walked out half way through to get to the NAAFI before it closed, leaving Laurence Olivier and Joan Fontaine to get on with it.

In July or August 1940, together with two other fusiliers, I went to see *Northwest Passage* in Dover. We had seats in the circle, and the cinema was packed, mostly with servicemen. Somewhere along the trail with Spencer Tracy there was a terrific crash. The cinema shook and bits of plaster fell from the ceiling. The lights were switched on and the manager came out on the stage. He apologized for the interruption, explaining that the Germans had started shelling the town. Did we want the show to go on, or did we prefer to go to the shelters? Everyone yelled out in favour of getting on with the show. Unlike an air raid, shelling in the Dover area was desultory, and it was unlikely that the Germans would lob over more than a shell or two every fifteen minutes.

During the rest of the performance there were several hefty thumps somewhere outside, and when the show was over and we went out into the night we were not surprised to find that a building almost opposite the cinema had been demolished. Looking back, it was not really worth risking one's neck to see *Northwest Passage*. I have seen better films.

A film I was enjoying but never got to see the end of was *The Fighting 69th* with James Cagney and Pat O'Brien, which I saw at the Warner, Leicester Square, while home on leave. An air raid started, the back of the cinema was blasted, and, unlike the time at Dover, the audience had to clear out without any option. There was a reissue of the film in 1948, but I missed it.

I know I saw Gary Cooper with Ingrid Bergman in Paramount's *For Whom the Bell Tolls*: there is an entry in my film diary. But I can recall little about it. Could I have fallen asleep in the cinema? Possibly. I frequently did. I know I saw many westerns at garrison cinemas, but there again my mind is a blank. I often used to go to the garrison cinema in Aldershot. It was free, so we lost nothing if we did not like the film and walked out to pass an hour or two at a nearby NAAFI or soldiers' canteen.

I believe it was in Barnstaple or Bideford that I saw Orson Welles in *Citizen Kane*. I was persuaded to see the film by an intellectual and very erudite fusilier, an ex-teacher, who, it was reputed, had been turned down at an OCTU interview for saying "shit" to an officer. He had seen the film in London whilst on leave and thought I ought to see it. I suffered for the most part in silence, although not everyone in the audience was so polite, but after we came out of the cinema I wanted to "do" my intellectual friend and said he ought to give me my money back. He said I was a Philistine and that he would buy me a tea instead. So we went to the Methodist Canteen for the Forces where a good cup of tea cost a halfpenny (old money) and a "wad" was a penny, and he told me why *Citizen Kane* was an outstanding film. When he saw I was not at all impressed he said "shit" to me. He might have made an officer: but a gentleman? – never!

I must have been a glutton for punishment, for I subsequently saw two more Welles films, *The Magnificent Ambersons* and *Journey into Fear*. I liked neither. Yet the ideas Orson Welles brought to filming were novel and truly experimental and must have influenced the work of most film-makers. First-person narration, wide-angled photography, and sharp focus were features of Welles' movies. The dramatic chiaroscuro of his camera work, which to many appeared old-fashioned at first, was considered revolutionary by professional photographers, who were quick to emulate his technique. Soon one could not see the wood for the trees. Angles, lighting, and technique became more important than story and dialogue. The means had become the end, and the result was confusion and boredom.

In South-East Asia, Army kinema units brought the cinema to the troops, often giving shows in the open, in fields, parade grounds, or jungle clearings, and servicemen gathered round higgledy-piggledy sitting on the ground or on boxes they brought with them. Indian troops often sat at the rear of the transparent screen watching the film projected through to the reverse side. When British troops went to see a film in the Indian lines they watched the reverse side of the screen.

The best film shows were those of the U.S. Forces, and we considered ourselves lucky to be with American troops. They were shown the latest films direct from Hollywood. At sundown we would gather around the screen expectantly. The sun descended swiftly in India, and it was soon dark enough for the picture show to commence. We would sit comfortably in the open on a hot tropical night and watch a training film and then the latest gift from Hollywood, eating mandarins and plantains, keeping our tin mugs handy while waiting for the *char-wallah* to come round with hot, sweet tea and little sugar

Spencer Tracy.

115

Orson Welles in *The Stranger* (1946).

cakes costing a few annas. I remember one film I saw on the racecourse outside Delhi which went down well with our tea and cake. It was *Bring on the Girls* with Eddie Bracken, Veronica Lake, and Sonny Tufts.

I also saw a film about the Doolittle raid on Tokyo while I was in India. This was *Thirty Seconds over Tokyo* with Van Johnson and Robert Walker, and starred Spencer Tracy as Lieutenant-Colonel James H. Doolittle. Early in 1944 there was something of a "flap" in military circles in New Delhi when a peanut-wallah outside the leading cinema in Connaught Square was found to be making the

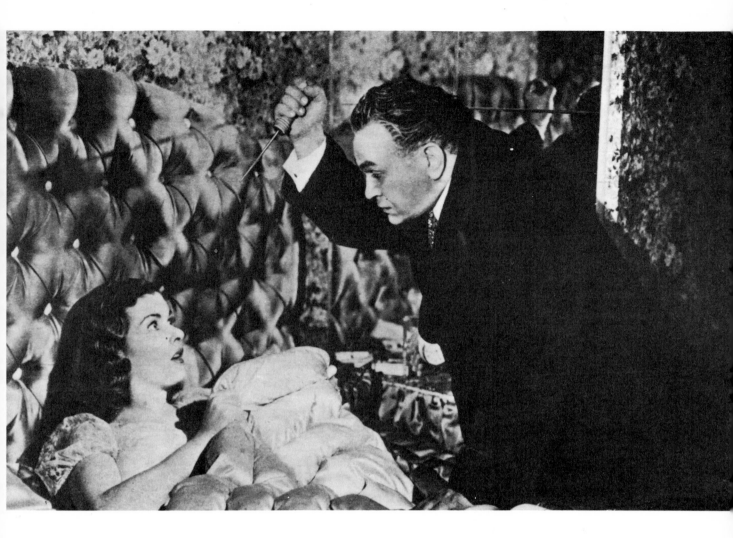

Edward G. Robinson and
Joan Bennett in *Scarlet Street*.

cornet-shaped bags for his peanuts from classified papers from the Secretariat.

I think the last film I saw in India was *Hangover Square* with Laird Cregar, Linda Darnell, and George Sanders. Laird Cregar played the part of a composer who just simply had to murder anybody who he considered murdered music. Such a man would have a busy time today.

Once at the Wales cinema in Kandy, Ceylon, some monkeys climbed onto the corrugated iron roof during a performance. It sounded like an avalanche. The noise became so bad we had to come out of the cinema and throw coconut shells at the monkeys to drive them away. They thought it was a game, and we enjoyed the monkeys' antics more than the film, which was called *Bathing Beauty* and featured Red Skelton and Esther Williams.

Whilst on leave in Colombo a party of us including submariners and frogmen hired a dozen or more rickshaws and were pulled along at a lively speed in convoy, whooping and cheering, to the New Olympia Cinema where we saw *A Game of Death* with John Loder as a big-game hunter shipwrecked on an island owned by a maniac who got his jollies hunting human prey.

117

Vincent Price, Gene Tierney, Clifton Webb, and Dana Andrews in *Laura*.

A film that raised a storm in 1945, especially among British servicemen, was *Objective Burma* starring Errol Flynn and featuring George Tobias, Henry Hull, William Prince, and Dick Erdman – a travesty based on the Chindit expedition of Wingate. Although the film was entertaining, it should never have been shown to SEAC troops or released to cinemas in Britain at the time, since it implied that the Burma operation was practically an all-American show and gave very small credit indeed to the British. Even American servicemen in China, Burma, and India recognized the gross unfairness of the film and gave it the bird.

In the days of continuous cinema performances patrons could and did come into a cinema at any time during a show, grope their way to seats to the discomfort of others, and see the programme round to the point where they had come in, taking in the other feature film and the newsreel on the way. This, of course, meant seeing the end of the film before the beginning, putting the cart before the horse, which could spoil the plot, timing, and suspense of any movie. It was worse than reading the end of a book before the beginning. In the old days we did not worry too much about that, since we were glad to get a seat at all. But it mattered more towards the end of the war and afterwards, when musicals, patriotic mush, documentaries, and schmaltz had given way to a spate of thrillers, horror films, and tough detective mysteries.

Scarlet Street starred Edward G. Robinson in an unfamiliar role, as a diffident bank clerk whose infatuation for a worthless girl, played by Joan Bennett, led him to dip into the bank's coffers to lavish goodies such as diamonds and mink on his love. But then he discovered that she was the willing tool of a cheap, despicable crook with a big sneer, admirably played by who else but the hateful

118

Dan Duryea. Mad with jealousy Edward G. stabbed his love with an icepick, leaving Dan to carry the can. All ended dismally.

For *Mildred Pierce*, the ingredients were lashings of blackmail, murder, larceny, and lust. Joan Crawford played the doting mother of a hard-nosed daughter, Ann Blyth, who had an affair with her slimy step-father (Zachary Scott) and then did him in. The almost incestuous affair and the nastiness of the characters was the foil for an over-emotional and over-emphasized performance by Joan Crawford, which won her an Oscar.

In James Cain's *The Postman Always Rings Twice*, John Garfield played the part of a drifter who drifted into the life of a gas station proprietor's wife who seduced him, which was not very difficult to believe as the wife was played by Lana Turner. She persuaded him to kill her husband, and he did so at the second attempt. But, of course, no good came of it, and retribution caught up with them in the way it was bound to in films of the forties.

Otto Preminger's *Fallen Angel* was a tight story of sex and murder in a small town. Dana Andrews played another drifter, who married good girl Alice Faye for money then ran off with bad girl Linda Darnell. Linda was murdered in sordid circumstances and Dana was prime suspect.

Following his success as the tough private eye Philip Marlowe in Raymond Chandler's *Farewell My Lovely,* Dick Powell continued to be tough in *Cornered* as a Canadian air ace searching for the Nazis who had killed his French wife, the search taking him from France to Switzerland and thence Argentina before he caught up with his quarry. Another Raymond Chandler story was *The Blue Dahlia* with Alan Ladd back from the wars to find that his dipsomaniac wife had been responsible for the death of their son. She was murdered and the plot thickened. William Bendix as an ex-airman with a hole in his head suited the part well.

A macabre thriller was R.K.O. Radio's *The Spiral Staircase*, in which Dorothy McGuire played a deaf mute pursued by a psychopath whose mission in life was to do away with girls with some physical defect as he believed all women ought to be perfect. To believe that, he had to be mad.

Laura, directed by Otto Preminger and starring Dana Andrews and Gene Tierney, was a psychological "whodunnit" in which acerbic, kipper-under-the-nose Clifton Webb returned to the screen after a long absence. Gene Tierney was never more than a chocolate box beauty, Dana was never able to rid himself of his pained expression, but Webb's contrived nastiness was a novelty on the screen.

Metro-Goldwyn-Mayer's *Music for the Millions*, one of the best musicals of 1945, had Jose Iturbi playing and conducting popular classics by Debussy, Chopin, Beethoven, and other great composers. The story-line was practically invisible, but a strong cast which included Margaret O'Brien, June Allyson, the irrepressible "Schnozzle" Durante, Marie Wilson, and Larry Adler made up for

Two pianists: Jose Iturbi and Jimmy Durante in *Music for Millions*.

this somewhat. Another M.G.M. musical was *Meet Me in St. Louis* with Judy Garland. Set at the turn of the century, the film was a light froth of colourful costumes and mellifluous melodies. It was directed by Vincente Minnelli.

R.K.O. Radio released *The Princess and the Pirate*, a Technicolor spectacular starring Bob Hope, which was advertised as being uproariously funny, though as is frequently the case it was not quite as advertised. But Bob was back with his old partners Bing Crosby and Dorothy Lamour to take Paramount's *Road to Utopia* in search of a gold-mine, and it was Paramount who found it, at the box office. Slaphappy comedy was provided in films with Abbott and Costello, Olsen and Johnson, and Laurel and Hardy: hardly more subtle was Warner's screen version of the comedy thriller *Arsenic and Old Lace*, directed by Frank Capra and starring Cary Grant. In this well-known story Cary found himself involved with two dear old aunts whose predilection for murder left bodies stashed away in odd places all over the house.

Twentieth Century-Fox presented *The Keys of the Kingdom*, adapted from A. J. Cronin's novel about a young Catholic priest who, failing to succeed in his calling in England, went to China as a missionary and found fulfilment. The new star who played the priest was Gregory Peck. With him were Thomas Mitchell, Vincent Price, and young Roddy McDowell.

120

Judy Garland.

Walter Brennan, Bob Hope, and Virginia Mayo in *The Princess and the Pirate*.

Another film from Twentieth Century-Fox was John Hersey's story *A Bell for Adano*. This was about an American-Italian in the Civil Affairs Administration of the American Army, Major Joppolo, who was given the task of restoring normalcy to the recently captured Sicilian town of Adano. Joppolo took his task so much to heart that he countermanded a superior's stupid order which would have upset the life of the town, and was removed and disgraced for his trouble. John Hodiak played Joppolo with as much honesty and feeling as could possibly be mustered for such an artificial role, and William Bendix went along with him as best he could. The bell for Adano? That was one to replace the bell taken away from the town by bad Italians.

None but the Lonely Heart was the screen adaptation of Richard Llewellyn's story of Cockneys, and was made and played almost entirely by Americans. British-born Cary Grant played a young man oppressed by squalor and vice who turned to crime as a way out. American Cockneys! Cor! What next? Knees up Momma Brown!

M.G.M. came up with a screen version of *The Picture of Dorian Gray*, about a man who retained eternal youth while the ravages

122

Cary Grant, Jean Adair,
Edward Everett Horton,
Josephine Hull, and Peter
Lorre in *Arsenic and Old Lace*.

of his life of vice, depravity, and corruption showed only on his portrait hidden in his attic. The film kept vaguely to Wilde's original story, but veered sharply away from controversial points that might have contravened the high-minded cinema ethics of the times. Hurd Hatfield was Dorian, and George Sanders, Donna Reed, Angela Lansbury, and Peter Lawford pitched in with their support.

In *Blood on the Sun* James Cagney gave a spirited performance as a newspaper reporter who, all on his own, way back in 1928, unearthed Japanese plans for the future conquest of America. With his ever-handy fists, pugnacious personality, and dogged determination Cagney managed to put it over on those wily pre–Pearl Harbor Orientals. Sylvia Sidney and Wallace Ford were in there with him.

It was back to the psychological stakes for United Artists with *Dark Waters*, featuring Merle Oberon, Franchot Tone, Thomas Mitchell, and Fay Bainter. Louisiana swampland was the background for this grey tale of murder and terror in which a doctor fights to save the sanity of a girl tortured by dark shadows trying to stifle her. Ugh! and ugh, again!

123

Gregory Peck as the priest
in *The Keys of the Kingdom*.

Bette Davis and Claude Rains starred in *Mrs. Skeffington*, the dreary story of a vain, supercilious, selfish woman who married a simple unselfish man who happened to be Jewish, and for his trouble made his life one of unrelieved misery.

Fresh from his exploits in *Objective Burma*, the irrepressible Errol Flynn turned up in Warner Brothers' *San Antonio* as a tough, quick-on-the-draw rancher who went south of the border to round up the rustlers who had shot him. Alexis Smith was the night-club singer working for the villain. The film was good swashbuckling Errol Flynn stuff, and Errol could swash better than most.

In 1946, psychological thrillers were still coming in hot and strong. Typical was *Shock*, a murder mystery labelled psychological to drum up interest in what was really just a pedestrian drama. A psychiatrist with a passion for one of his nurses bashed in his wife's

Gene Tierney in *A Bell for Adano*.

skull with a prosaic candlestick and crammed her body into the boot of his car in order to remove it to his house in the country. But a neighbour awaiting her soldier husband's return from the wars had witnessed the fell deed and, overcome by the shock, went into a traumatic trance. Returning to find her still in this cataleptic state, her husband, naturally, was extremely put out. He sought the help of a psychiatrist. Who else? In his private clinic the doctor soon discovered from the drug-induced babblings of his pretty patient that she had witnessed a murder, and in one of her more lucid moments, horror upon horror, she realized that the doctor was the murderer; and he knew she knew, and he knew he had to nobble her. But how? A doctor's choice is wide, especially if he is played by Vincent Price. So he set about his task with the usual hypnotic suggestion bit, but it proved unsatisfactory for his purpose so he decided to give the sleeping beauty an overdose of insulin, a drug which we were given to understand was used for psychotic disorders. With all his devious planning the brilliant doctor paused to strangle, in a mundane fashion, the nurse who had been the start of all his troubles. Lynn Bari was the nurse. The film was from Twentieth Century-Fox.

Another Twentieth Century-Fox film was *Dragonwyck*, directed by Joseph L. Mankiewicz and starring Gene Tierney, Walter Huston, and the indefatigable Vincent Price. Set in the 1850s, this was about a wealthy and egotistical landowner who murdered his wife when she was unable to give him a son. When a girl who came all the way from Connecticut to be his second wife was also unable to do the

125

Cary Grant, Ethel Barrymore, and Barry Fitzgerald in *None but the Lonely Heart*.

James Cagney raises his hand to Sylvia Sidney in *Blood on the Sun*.

126

Bette Davis.

desired trick, he tried to dispose of her too. The setting was a massive, gloomy, turreted mansion on the Hudson, where ghosts flitted back and forth in an atmosphere of weird brooding. The gloom spread to the audience.

Warner Brothers' *Night and Day* was the highly Technicolored story of composer Cole Porter, from his early days at Yale University, where he was studying law, then his switch from law to music, on through his service with the French Army in World War I, to his eventual musical success. Background music included such hit numbers as "Begin the Beguine", "My Heart Belongs to Daddy", "What Is This Thing Called Love", and the classic "Night and Day" that gave the film its title. Urbane Cary Grant played Porter, Alexis Smith portrayed Ginny Simms, and Monty Woolley, who had known Porter in the old days, played himself.

Saratoga Trunk, based on the novel by Edna Ferber, was also a Warner Brothers release and starred Gary Cooper and Ingrid Bergman. Gary was a Texas gambler allied with Ingrid, who played the unscrupulous, illegitimate Creole beauty Clio Dulaine, who was seeking a rich husband and revenge against a background of snobbery and vice in New Orleans circa 1870. Ferber's novel was a Pulitzer Prize winner, but the film deserved no accolades.

Another film from Warner Brothers was *The Big Sleep*, produced by Howard Hawks and starring box office favourites Humphrey Bogart and Lauren Bacall. Scripted by William Faulkner from Raymond Chandler's novel, the confused plot was about a private detective hired to track down a blackmailer, only to find he had been murdered. Racy dialogue and convincing acting helped to drag this puzzler out of the doldrums. Eagle-Lion had a go at Shaw's *Caesar and Cleopatra* to the tune of £1,500,000, which even in these days of super-inflation is not hay. It took two years to make this spectacular; it ran for two hours, and was dismissed by many of the critics in two minutes as tedious, verbose, and hammed up in spots. Yet it was intensely interesting because of its spectacle, the occasional flashes of Shavian wit, and the glittering cast, which included Stewart Granger, Flora Robson, Francis L. Sullivan, Basil Sidney, and others, and read like a "who's who" in British films of a year or two later.

In *Monsieur Beaucaire* Bob Hope appeared complete with powdered wig, silk stockings, and knee breeches, which was a laugh for a start. In this adaptation of a Booth Tarkington novel Hope took the part of the barber who impersonated a French nobleman in order to marry a Spanish princess, thus hoping to avert a war.

Considered one of the best British pictures of 1946 was Cineguild's adaptation of Noël Coward's play *Brief Encounter*, superbly and sensitively directed by David Lean. This was about an affair that never was between a reasonably happy suburban housewife and a married doctor who met by chance at a railway station; their attraction for each other, their empathy, and their inevitable parting with its wistful

Stewart Granger, Vivien
Leigh, Basil Sydney, and
Claude Rains in *Caesar and
Cleopatra*.

realism. Celia Johnson was perfect as the housewife, and Trevor Howard was no less perfect as the doctor.

It was in 1946 that Joseph I. Breen, America's administrator of the American Film Production Code, visited England with the intention of explaining to British film producers what could be said in, and what should be omitted from, British films if the producers wished to avoid trouble with the American film censors. At the time words like "bloody" could mean a ban on British films in America, and words like "fag", which has a different connotation in America, had to be avoided at all costs. Even Shakespeare could mean controversy with the puritanical American censors. Too much realism in film dialogue was not yet acceptable in England or America, and even in war films, the oaths and expletives put into the mouths of tough servicemen were usually pallid euphemisms enough to make an old soldier squirm in his seat.

According to their movie titles, by 1947 the Yanks had been practically everywhere. Robert Taylor starred in *A Yank at Oxford* in 1937. In 1941 Tyrone Power and Betty Grable showed us *A Yank in the R.A.F.*, Mickey Rooney was *A Yank at Eton* in 1942, and in 1946 Anna Neagle and Dean Jagger were in *A Yank in London*. So it was no surprise when in 1947 Valentina Cortese and Leo Dale appeared in *A Yank in Rome*.

Deborah Kerr and Trevor Howard starred in a comedy spy thriller called *The Adventurers*, which was about an Irish girl who naturally hated England and was naïve enough to become the unwitting instrument of Nazi agents. The film had its fleeting moments, but none worth reliving.

More meaty was Paramount's *California*, starring Barbara Stanwyck and Ray Milland. The setting was California in its early Wild West days, when mustachioed villains wearing metal armbands and fancy vests not unnaturally had vested interests which meant they did not want the territory to become a state of the Union. Usually urbane Ray Milland looked a little less at home in the spiky atmosphere of the Far West than did tough Barbara Stanwyck.

A big, wide-roaming romantic western epic was *Duel in the Sun* with Gregory Peck, Jennifer Jones, Joseph Cotten, Lionel Barrymore, Walter Huston, and Lillian Gish. Broadly based on a Nevil Shute novel, it told of the adventures of a half-breed Indian girl who came to live in the house of a wealthy cattle baron and upset the applecart when both his sons fell in love with her. The plot unfolded against a background of the cattlemen's resistance to the encroaching railroads in the 1880s. Because of storms of protest from religious bodies, David Selznick was reputed to have made forty-six cuts in the film.

United Artists released *The Fabulous Dorseys* at the beginning of 1947. It was the biography, more or less – probably less – of the famous bandleaders who, publicity had it, scrapped with each other as they swung to the top of the tree. The plot was thin as a reed, the music good of its time, and Janet Blair was very pretty.

The Farmer's Daughter with Loretta Young, Joseph Cotten, and Ethel Barrymore was an R.K.O. Radio comedy drama about a forthright Swedish immigrant working in the U.S.A. as a servant girl who sallied forth to contest a seat in Congress and before long had rallied just about everyone round her flag. Bags of patriotism and tub-thumping provided comedy that was not meant.

One of the better films of the 1947 crop was *Boomerang* from Twentieth Century-Fox, directed by the masterly Elia Kazan and starring the ubiquitous Dana Andrews, with Jane Wyatt and Lee J. Cobb. This concerned a prosecuting attorney who did not believe the case of the state. Based on a true story, the film was presented in the style of a documentary.

Gregory Peck, the immaculate Joan Bennett, and Robert Preston were in United Artists' *The Macomber Affair*. The film, based on Hemingway's story, was about the triangle of husband, wife, and guide on safari in deepest Africa. Gregory Peck was cool, restrained, and implacable as the guide.

Errol Flynn, still a scapegoat because of *Objective Burma*, soothed his critics when in 1947 he married Nora Eddington, whom he was said to have met in a cigar store. But they started sharpening their quills again when it was announced that he was starting *The Adventures of Don Juan*. Rumour had it that he had to outkiss John Barrymore, the great lover, who had played the role years before and had notched up a record 191 kisses in his epic performance. Confident Errol was undaunted, despite his critics waiting ready to pounce.

Efforts while they were in England in 1947 to persuade Laurel and Hardy to make a British film were in vain. The two comedians made a number of personal appearances, and one function they performed which provided a good deal of amusement was the re-opening ceremony of the famous Romney, Hythe and Dymchurch Railway in Kent, which had been used in the war for mobile anti-aircraft batteries.

A busy young star was Dennis Price, who appeared with Margaret Lockwood in *Hungry Hill*, the story of two Irish families whose long feud brought poverty and ruin to both sides. Dreary, long-winded, and disjointed like the "troubles", the film did have a few shining moments.

Metro-Goldwyn-Mayer's *High Barbaree* with Van Johnson, June Allyson, and Thomas Mitchell was about two baled-out airmen floating on a raft in the Pacific. While one groaned helplessly, and the audience with him, the other bored him and the audience with the story of his life.

Twentieth Century-Fox came up with *Homestretch*, starring Cornel Wilde and Maureen O'Hara. It was a film that may have brought a little joy to horse-racing enthusiasts, but it was a non-starter for everyone else. Set against colourful backgrounds of racing from Ascot

Mickey Rooney.

Lauren Bacall in her screen debut with Bogart in *To Have and Have Not*.

in Britain to Churchill Downs in the U.S.A., the pathetically thin story-line of *Homestretch* was the two-way stretch between a keen race-horse owner and his not at all horsey wife.

Homecoming was another film from Twentieth Century-Fox and starred Clark Gable, as the husband of Anne Baxter, having a hot-box-office affair with Lana Turner in flashbacks. The good cast could do little to put life into this boring film with a World War II background.

No more entertaining was *The Long Night*, an R.K.O. Radio release with Henry Fonda, Barbara Bel Geddes, and Vincent Price, who deserved a better fate than playing in this tedious and contrived drama. The story-line, only a little less familiar then than it is now, was about a murderer who hid away in a sordid hotel while his girl-friend went through the whole gamut of emotions to persuade him to give himself up. It was a pity she did not succeed right at the beginning of the film and so save the audience an hour and a half of boredom.

Gunfighters, starring the always popular, always tough Randolph Scott, with Barbara Britton and Forrest Tucker, was the old western theme that is still going strong, of a gunslinger who wants to hang up his guns but cannot keep them on the hook. He was forced to take them down when he found himself slap in the middle of a range war and he was back in business. Bang! Bang!

Only blind lovers of Rimsky-Korsakov's music and aficionados of spectacular film-settings could have stuck out the 106 minutes of Universal's utterly boring *Song of Scheherazade*, starring Yvonne De Carlo, Jean-Pierre Aumont, and Brian Donlevy. The unlikely plot purported to be based on the life of the great Russian composer and his love for a dancing girl named Cara. There was no need to bring on the dancing girls.

Devotees of jazz music liked United Artists' *New Orleans* with Arturo Cordova and Dorothy Patrick. There was good music from Louis Armstrong, Woody Herman and Billie Holliday, so what did it matter if the story was dull if you liked jazz?

For anybody in 1947 who could still be tuned in by a "Thin Man" picture there was Metro-Goldwyn-Mayer's *Song of the Thin Man* with the old firm of William Powell and the lady with the upswept nose, Myrna Loy. In this offering suave William as Nick and pretty Myrna as Nora moved in ever-decreasing circles, especially jazz circles, to run a murderer to earth. Threadbare in places, the fabric of the plot managed to give the famous couple opportunities for some slick dialogue.

A prison break, a sadistic guard, and the whole prison bit was laid on thick for Burt Lancaster in Universal's *Brute Force*, with Yvonne De Carlo, Howard Duff, and Hume Cronyn to help the action along. Even way back in 1947, prison pictures were beginning to pall, but within the narrow limits of prison walls the film scored a few points.

Captain Boycott, a British picture with Stewart Granger, Kathleen

Yvonne De Carlo making her debut in *Salome Where She Danced* (1944).

Ryan, and Cecil Parker, loosely followed the true story of a wealthy landowner in old Ireland who threatened his tenants with eviction. Being Irish, the tenants fought back with gusto. A historical melodrama, the film had breadth and pace and was well acted.

R.K.O. Radio's *Magic Town* was a film about a small town boosted by a public opinion pollster as reflecting exactly what always turned out to be statistically correct. This did the once quiet little town no good at all. Plum-in-his-mouth James Stewart bumbled and swallowed, and Jane Wyman went along for the ride. This film was supposed to be funny. It was not.

There was no novelty in Eagle-Lion's *Love from a Stranger* with Sylvia Sidney and John Hodiak. A suspense drama, it was about a girl who married a man and then suspected him of being the mad strangler the police were looking for, who intended to make her his next victim.

Far better was Monogram's *The Gangster* with Barry Sullivan, Belita, and John Ireland, a well-presented psychological study of a hoodlum whose inner conflicts resulted in his losing his nerve, being deserted by his gang, and finally being gunned down by rival mobsters.

Released by Universal in 1947, another picture of a raw side of life was *Body and Soul* starring stocky John Garfield, better looking and nearly as tough as Cagney. The film, publicized as one of the best boxing films ever made, was, as usual, about a boy from the

slums fighting his way to the top despite all the blandishments of
crooks and females on the make. The boxing scenes were reasonably
realistic to those who knew nothing about boxing, but leading lady
Lilli Palmer's acting was realistic enough for everybody.

Public opinion polls, for what they were worth in 1947, seemed
to indicate that British cinemagoers thought they could well do without
American films, and perhaps influenced by this, the Labour Government thought it could save precious dollars by slapping a massive
import duty on American movies. The result was disastrous, and in
the seven months that the import duty imposition lasted, from August
1947 to March 1948, the British cinema trade was nearly crippled.

Metro-Goldwyn-Mayer's *Cass Timberlane*, starring Spencer Tracy,
Lana Turner, and Zachary Scott, was a fairly faithful screen adaptation
of the Sinclair Lewis novel. The story centred about the problems
of a straight judge in the American Midwest who married a younger
woman then had to "go some" to keep pace with his immature but
lively bride.

Barry Fitzgerald, Howard Duff, and Doris Hart starred in Universal's *The Naked City*, a conventional story about a police investigation
into the murder of a girl. The stark backgrounds of New York City
in the raw raised the film right out of a rut, and it was the basis
for a successful TV series.

Another Universal film was *Woman's Vengeance* by Aldous Huxley,
starring Charles Boyer, the heart-throb with the sexy French accent;
Ann Blyth; and Jessica Tandy. The film was about a married man's
affair with a younger woman and his arrest and trial for murder
when his wife was poisoned.

Saigon from Paramount starred Alan Ladd and Veronica Lake in
an ineffective tale about black marketeering and intrigue before
American involvement in Vietnam, and as a film it was "ho-hum".

James Mason, Barbara Bel Geddes, and Robert Ryan starred in
Metro-Goldwyn-Mayer's melodrama *Caught*, which was about a

135

Barry Fitzgerald and Bing
Crosby starred as priests in
Going My Way (1944).

model who married a neurotic millionaire, and the young doctor who helped her in her trouble.

Big stars do not always make a big film, nor does "big" in the title. Some "big" titles of 1948 were Eagle-Lion's *The Big Cat* with Preston Foster, Lon McCallister, and Forrest Tucker; M.G.M.'s *Big City* with Margaret O'Brien, Danny Thomas, and Preston Foster; Warner Brothers' *The Big Punch* with Wayne Morris and Lois Maxwell; Paramount's *Big Town Scandal* with Philip Reed and Hilary Brooks; and Paramount's *The Big Clock* with Ray Milland and Charles Laughton. *The Big Cat* was an action adventure film about a city man helping to track down a killer cougar in mountain country. Whatever the neatly packaged *Big City* was trying to say was lost in weepy slush and schmaltz. It was about an orphan adopted jointly by a Catholic, a Protestant, and a Jew. *The Big Punch* lacked any punch and was just a big bore. *Big Town Scandal* was nothing to write home about. *The Big Clock* was a suspenseful mystery story about a man who, following clues to the identity of a murderer, found that they led to him.

Universal's presentation of *Hamlet* with Laurence Olivier, Jean Simmons, Basil Sydney, and Eileen Herlie did true justice to Shakespeare's greatest play, and Olivier's portrayal of the Danish prince brought to life the true essence of the tragedy and made the film a classic.

Not so classic was R.K.O.'s *Joan of Arc* with Ingrid Bergman, Jose Ferrer, Francis L. Sullivan, and Ward Bond. This mammoth film, which was boosted by the Press and won a Special Academy Award, was adapted from Maxwell Anderson's stage play *Maid of Orleans*, and based precariously on the life of a simple French farm girl. Jockeyed into the position of leader of the French armies against the English she was finally captured and burned at the stake. The film aroused no fervour despite Ingrid's saintliness.

Key Largo from Warner Brothers had a strong cast in Humphrey Bogart, Lauren Bacall, Edward G. Robinson, Lionel Barrymore, and Claire Trevor, and a top-rate director in John Huston. Yet this strange gangster melodrama set in the storm-swept Florida Keys was just adequate entertainment, nothing more.

Robert Louis Stevenson's story of the Wars of the Roses, *The Black Arrow*, was brought to the screen by Columbia and starred Louis Hayward and Janet Blair. Louis Hayward, not quite as competent a swashbuckler as Errol Flynn, nevertheless managed to keep up the pace of the adventure in fine style.

Warner Brothers' *Johnny Belinda* with Lew Ayres and Jane Wyman won an Oscar for Jane. She played a deaf mute befriended by a compassionate doctor in a sensitive and moving story.

It took just over three years to get from *Blood on the Sun* to the inevitable *Blood on the Moon*. Robert Mitchum, Barbara Bel Geddes, and Robert Preston starred in this R.K.O. Radio western. Poker-faced Mitchum played a poker-faced cowpoke in conflict with a girl and

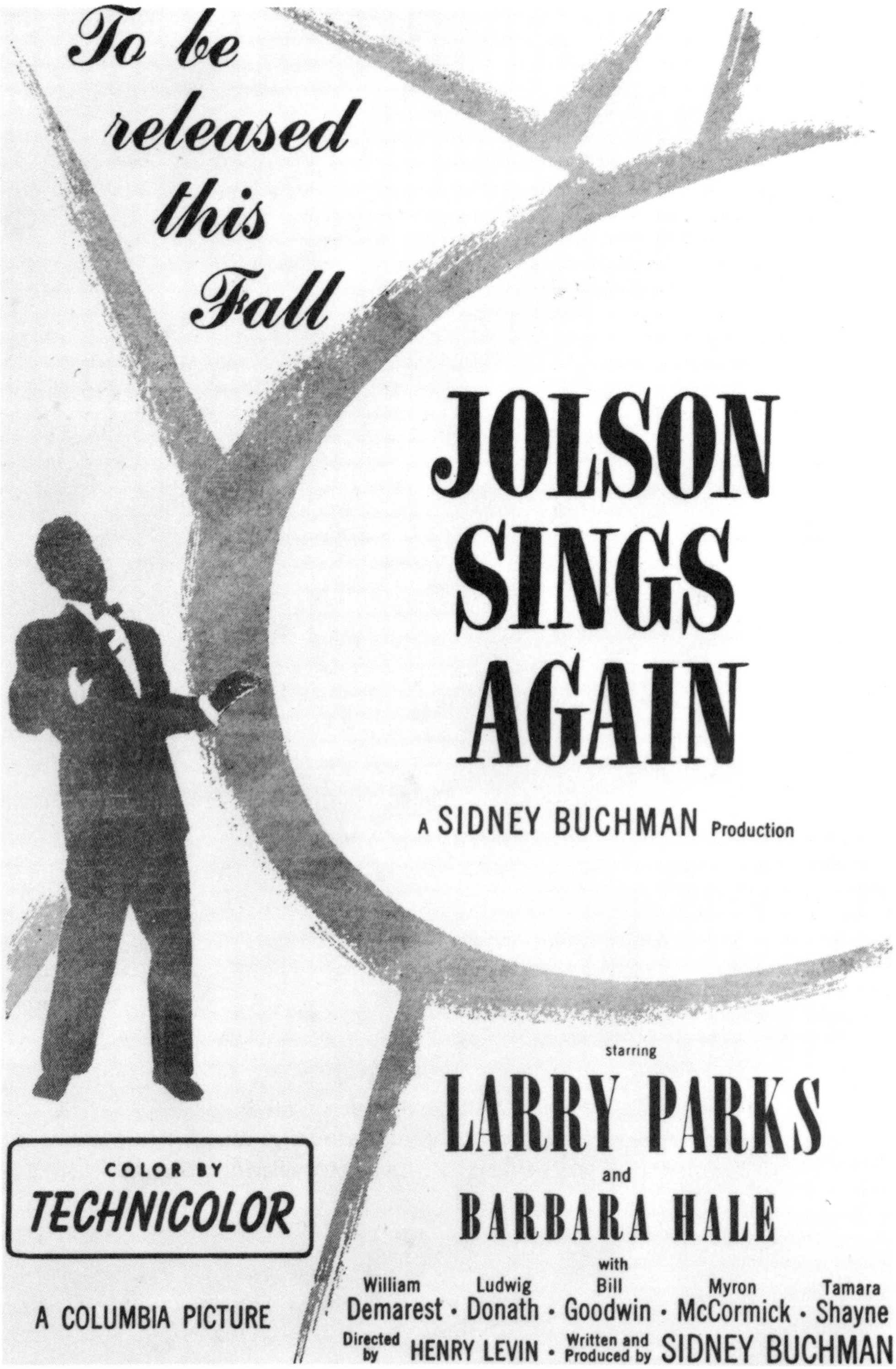
To be released this Fall
JOLSON SINGS AGAIN
A SIDNEY BUCHMAN Production
starring
LARRY PARKS
and
BARBARA HALE
with
William Demarest · Ludwig Donath · Bill Goodwin · Myron McCormick · Tamara Shayne
Directed by HENRY LEVIN · Written and Produced by SIDNEY BUCHMAN
COLOR BY TECHNICOLOR
A COLUMBIA PICTURE

her dad. The hoary story was a little fresher in those days. So was Mitchum, which does not mean he was a better actor then. He has matured, like good cheese.

In January 1949, Metro-Goldwyn-Mayer released *Three Godfathers* directed by John Ford and starring John Wayne, Pedro Armendariz, and Harry Carey, Jr. It was about three outlaws way out west who while on the run across the desert find an abandoned child. John Wayne was looming large.

Entirely different was Metro-Goldwyn-Mayer's *The Secret Garden*, which was about two children, played by Margaret O'Brien and Dean Stockwell, who discovered a secret and magic garden. The eerie atmosphere and suspense was well done, and the children performed better than usual.

Warner Brother's hot property, pre-political Ronald Reagan, starred with Patricia Neal and Jack Carson in the screen version of the stage comedy *John Loves Mary*. It was about the attempts of a soldier returning from World War II to sneak his bride into the U.S.A. while his fiancée is trying to pin him down to marriage. It was contrived and painfully unfunny and would not win Reagan any votes nowadays.

Johnnies-on-the-spot included George Raft playing his set-piece role of a sloe-eyed hoodlum but this time on the side of the law as an undercover agent trying to bring to book an international smuggling ring. In *Johnny Stool Pigeon*, Howard Duff as an ex-con did likewise to expose a dope ring. Just for the record *Johnny Holliday* with William Bendix and Stanley Clements was about a juvenile delinquent undergoing reformation at the Indiana Boys' School.

One of the best and most successful thrillers of the post-war era was *The Third Man* written by Graham Greene and directed by Carol Reed. To the haunting strains of the now familiar zither music of Anton Karas, Orson Welles, Joseph Cotten, Trevor Howard, and Valli played their parts to perfection. The plot centred on an American writer in Vienna who went to the funeral of an old friend, but soon discovered that the friend was very much alive and was, in fact, the ruthless leader of a vicious black market organization. Against silent streets, lively cafés, unusual backdrops, and the labyrinthine sewers of Vienna, the theme music heightened the atmosphere of suspense as monosodium glutamate heightens the flavour of food.

Twentieth Century-Fox's *Canadian Pacific* starred craggy-faced Randolph Scott as a tough, two-fisted surveyor who defied all odds and dangers to push a railway through hostile territory. With plenty of action to carry it along, and Jane Wyatt to provide the female interest, the film was far from outstanding. Even less outstanding, despite the notoriety of the colourful characters which gave the film its title, was *Calamity Jane and Sam Bass*, a tepid western. Howard Duff and Yvonne De Carlo did their best, but the odds were against them.

One of the biggest box-office draws in 1949 was the adaptation by

United Artists of Ring Lardner's *Champion*, starring Kirk Douglas, Marilyn Maxwell, Arthur Kennedy, Ruth Roman, and Lola Albright, and produced by Stanley Kramer. One of the most realistic films made of the fight business, it told the seamy story of the rise and fall of an unscrupulous and ambitious boxer and his destructive effect on his brother, wife, and friends.

Another film which was pretty raw stuff but well done was Twentieth Century-Fox's *The Snake Pit* with Olivia de Havilland, Mark Stevens, and Leo Genn. Adapted from a best-selling novel, it showed conditions in an overcrowded, understaffed mental hospital. Continuing in the sordid vein, *It Always Rains on Sundays*, a British picture starring Googie Withers and John McCallum, told a miserable tale about life and crime in the East End slums of London. The grim realism of the film was enough to make Googie forsake the East End and in later years become governor of a women's prison in a TV series.

As the decade ended, films were rolling off the stocks thick and fast. Cinemagoers would still have to queue at the local to see a well-publicized film, but if they failed to get in or preferred not to queue there was always a second and even a third choice at a cinema often just a few yards away in the same street. People saved their sweet ration to take to the cinema, and two or three pence bought a bag of peanuts. Little did cinemagoers realize that within the next decade they would be able to see the film for which they had queued – again and again and again on television.

The Bogey Legend

SOME YEARS AGO I WENT TO A BENEFIT SHOW, "U.S. A GOGO", at Madison Square Garden in New York. Among the stars appearing were Red Buttons, Johnny Carson, Joan Crawford, Robert Culp, Sammy Davis, Jr., Henry Fonda, and Peter Falk. The proceeds of the gala evening were to go towards providing entertainment for U.S. Armed Services all over the world. As we were leaving after the show I was introduced briefly to Allan Singer, a writer who was doing a piece on the show for a syndicate, and I was told that he had met just about everyone in Hollywood and up and down Broadway since the war.

The following evening, as we walked into the Carnegie, a popular "deli" on Seventh Avenue just north of Times Square, a voice called a greeting and there was Allan Singer beckoning us to the table where he was sitting alone. He invited us to join him, and soon we were talking about the previous evening's benefit show. In the course of the conversation Allan happened to mention that during the war he had been in Italy, where he had seen a number of U.S.O. shows, including one in which Humphrey Bogart had appeared. It transpired that Allan had interviewed Bogart several times in New York some years before, and he said that Bogey was even tougher in real life than in some of the roles he played on the screen. When Allan had asked him if there was any truth in a certain movie magazine article about him he replied, "Why ask me? I didn't write it." Asked whether he had enjoyed playing the part of the petty, craven, and incompetent Queeg in *The Caine Mutiny*, he replied, "Yes, I did. I met a lot of Queegs in the Navy." Bogey had served in the Navy in World War I.

Allan said that Bogart could cut interviewers down to size if he thought it necessary, with a single cutting remark. Once when a vapid female interviewer was coyly flaunting her charms to impress the imperturbable Bogey and asked with starry eyes and out-thrust breasts what was his ideal woman, he had replied sourly, "Well, let's put it this way, sister. I'm not a tit man." Another time, when a girl asked him the cliché question, "What do you think of women?" he barked right back, "First tell me what you think of men." To the earnest reporter who asked him what sort of message he liked

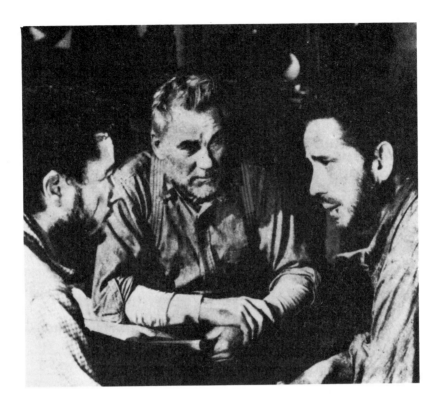

Humphrey Bogart.
Tim Holt, Walter Huston,
and Bogart as prospectors in
The Treasure of Sierra Madre.

to put across in his movies he replied, "Message? what message? If I want to send a message, I get through to Western Union." Asked if he believed in the sanctity of marriage, Bogey gave his questioner his well-known dead-pan swivel and said, "What sort of titty is that?"

I saw many early Bogart films, including his first gangster movie, *The Petrified Forest*, and probably liked them all. Among those I recall are *Angels with Dirty Faces*, *The Maltese Falcon*, *The Big Shot*, *Casablanca*, *The Big Sleep*, *The Two Mrs. Carrolls*, *The Treasure of Sierra Madre*; and *Key Largo*. I must admit that I did not recognize in Bogart a movie star who was to become a legend, even though he was voted one of the ten best money-making stars in the *Motion Picture Herald* Fame Poll in 1943, 1944, 1945, 1946, 1947, 1948, and 1949. It was only when I had seen some of his later movies and had seen some of his earlier ones again, including one of his best, *The Treasure of Sierra Madre*, in which he played a gold prospector, that I realized he was indeed a legend.

In 1938 when Humphrey Bogart was already well established as an actor, he took for his third wife a little blonde Broadway actress, Mayo Methot, who had also been married twice before. Mayo had made her reputation as an actress playing opposite George M. Cohan in *The Song and Dance Man*, and had subsequently appeared in several films without being anything in the way of a sensation. Bogart and Mayo were married at the home of Mel and Mary Baker in Bel Air. Mary Baker was Bogart's agent, and naturally accounts of the wedding and the subsequent goings on varied according to whatever publicity angles were being presented and what other agents, reporters, and columnists could contrive to squeeze out of it.

142

Whether a Hollywood wedding could be turned into a one- or three-ring circus depended a lot on the agents and publicity writers sniffing around for copy, but Bogey and Mayo had the fiery temperaments that provided plenty of fuel for the fire-raisers. For one thing, it was widely bruited that apart from packing a pretty nifty punch, Mayo was not averse to emphasizing her displeasure by hurling at a hapless offender whatever was to hand, be it a bottle, a chair, or a clock, and, it was said, her aim was very good.

Nobody was under any illusions about the marriage lasting forever. Bogart himself had been hopeful, to be sure, but not too sanguine about the chances of sailing into the everlasting sunshine of wedded bliss. He and his new partner were both two-time losers, and much of the gilt of marital novelty was already off the gingerbread for both of them. Years later Bogart confessed to what many already knew – that he and Mayo squabbled incessantly over just about everything, from the way the glasses were arranged in the drinks cupboard to the way books were arranged on the bookshelves. Bogart said, dead-pan, that more often than not she put them back on the shelves upside down because she did not know the difference. He did not approve of Mayo's political beliefs and preferences, and certainly did not care for her high regard for General MacArthur, who was anathema to him. She, for her part, took exception to some of his assertions, such as that he considered Ingrid Bergman to be the only lady in Hollywood.

Apparently, Bogart and Mayo did not worry too much about the reputation they had picked up for being Hollywood's prize pair of fighting cocks. They fought in public and boasted that they fought at home just as well without an audience. Hollywood took it for granted that the two love-birds were liable to haul off at any time and indulge in a bout of name-calling or a slugging match. Bogey called his peppery little sparring partner Sluggy, and what she called him from time to time was not at all flattering. Yet despite the belligerency Bogart displayed in his film roles, he seldom fought with

143

The Bogarts and Mr. and Mrs. Danny Kaye go night-clubbing.

anyone except Sluggy. When a columnist wrote, "The Bogarts opened their own second front at the 'Troc' last night", Mayo wanted Bogey to "knock the hell out of the author of that crack". But Bogart was reasonable about it and said, "Sluggy, it's a very funny crack and figuratively true." Sluggy was not placated and asked Bogey what the hell he meant by "figuratively".

On the wall over the bar in their home near Sunset Boulevard were displayed two framed items. One was a bill for breakages incurred when Bogey and Mayo had fought it out on the floor of the Algonquin Hotel. The other was an inimitable drawing made by Thurber after he had witnessed a fracas in which the Bogarts gave a valiant performance. According to the columnists, however, most of their best performances took place in their own home or in the privacy of hotel suites where sounds of their altercations, strident epithets followed by thuds and the sound of breaking glass, echoed through sedate corridors. As Dorothy Parker remarked, "Through their years together their neighbors were lulled to sleep by the sounds of breaking china and crashing glass." Hardly a lullaby.

Columnists would agree only that the Bogarts had been at it again, for their versions of what had actually happened depended largely on their own imaginations and what apt turns of phrase they could dream up for the occasion to provide slick copy. Once it was reported that Bogart and Mayo had had a set-to in which they clouted each other over the head with whisky bottles, winding up with Bogey tearing out of the house and going to a night club. As he was entering, the doorman told him that the back of his jacket was wet with what seemed to be blood. Mayo, it was said, had stabbed him in the back and he did not even know it. Another version of this famous battle was that Bogart called his agents one day and said, "Get over here, quick: she's stabbed me." Supposedly the agents had scurried to the Bogart residence, where Bogart was nonchalantly waiting with

144

Casablanca: Bogart and
Ingrid Bergman.

145

a slash in the back of his jacket through which blood was seeping, while Mayo stood by insisting hysterically that she had not done anything, despite the knife lying on the kitchen table. Strangely there is no record that when one of the agents asked him if it hurt, Bogart replied, "Only when I laugh."

When the Battling Bogarts, as they had come to be known, turned up in New York, they entertained a variety of people who wandered in and out of their apartment at all hours. There always seemed to be columnists, sportswriters, prize fighters, wrestlers, a host of actors and actresses, both big names and bit-parters, delivery boys from the "delis", tradesmen, and hangers-on.

One visitor was George Frazier, who was endeavouring to complete a profile on Bogart for *Life* magazine. Bogart seemed not to take this idea seriously and insisted it was he who was writing a profile on Frazier. He would phone Frazier and pretend to interview him. "Let's see," he would say, "you attended the Berlitz School of Languages on Fifth Avenue, where you played left tackle; then you went to Dale Carnegie's. You were sort of a dull creep, weren't you? What else?" On one occasion, it was said, he sent a telegram to Frazier's boss which read: "George Frazier's life story utterly impossible. He has absolutely no color. Nothing happened to him except he was born and his wife sleeps in the top of his pajamas. Suggest cancelling entire story."

Another tale which went the rounds concerned the time columnist Earl Wilson met the Bogarts at the 21 Club and Sluggy said, "We aren't very well this morning." Whereupon Bogey, looking lean, tough, and fit as a fiddle, started to groan, stopping only when the waiter brought him a double martini.

A patron leaned over Bogart and spoke down his ear. "Pal," he said, "can you tell me how a male broom and a female broom make little brushes?"

"You tell me," said Bogart without a smile.

"They sweep together," answered the patron, and went off chuckling, as pleased as a dog with two portions.

Bogart groaned. Then the penny dropped. "Hmm! Not bad," he

Advertisement for a wartime Bogart film.

Bogart with Robert Morley (left) and Peter Lorre. "Have I said something funny?"

said. "Not bad at all." Then he phoned John Steinbeck, the author, to try out the gag and thereafter a host of other friends before settling down to eat his meal.

Far from doing harm to his career Bogart's lack of inhibition increased his popularity and created a tough but pleasing image. His domestic life was untainted by spiteful gossip laced with unpleasant sexual connotations, because, by apparently concealing nothing, he stifled speculation. He did not drink secretly: he drank openly. He did not row with his wife where they could not be seen or heard: he quarrelled and fought for the world to see and hear. He was not a notorious woman-chaser, although Mayo, who was very jealous of her spouse, was convinced that he was always on the prowl. Once she actually had Bogey put under surveillance by a detective agency. According to Nunnally Johnson, "Bogey soon got wise to the fact that he was being tailed and by judicious inquiries was able to find out the agency for which his clumsy shadow worked, and he phoned them. 'This is Humphrey Bogart,' he said. 'You've got a man on my tail. Do me a favor. Would you please check with him and find out where I am? I'm lost.'"

Following the sensational success of *Casablanca*, Bogart and Mayo went on a U.S.O. tour of the war zones of Europe and North Africa. John Huston met the Bogarts when they came with the U.S.O. troupe to Italy while he was there with the Fifth Army. He saw Bogart at the Palace in Caserta in December 1943, surrounded by hundreds of battle-weary troops. Bogart had "shot the breeze" with the boys and kidded them as much as they kidded him. Huston said that the troops knew and loved Bogart and he enjoyed being with them.

Huston also mentioned an incident that had taken place in Oran

147

Partners in films and in life
–Lauren Bacall and
Bogart.

in North Africa. One night Mayo locked Bogart out of her room, and he began to break down the door just like the Bogart of the movies. An irate Army colonel had stormed up, yelling to Bogart to "cut it out" and demanding his name, rank, and serial number. According to Huston, Bogey, in U.S.O. uniform, despised "brass" on principle at all times, and in the case of this colonel it was hate at first sight. Bogart, who had served as an ordinary seaman on the warship *Leviathan* in World War I, yelled right back at the gallant colonel to go to goddamn hell and back and mind his own goddamn business. The colonel, said Huston, "nearly busted a gut".

The next day, as a guest of the U.S. Army, Bogart was carpeted, and it was suggested that he apologize to the apoplectic colonel for the scant respect he had shown him. Bogart nodded curtly at the colonel and said, "I didn't mean to insult the uniform. I just meant to insult you." He was unrepentant. The colonel said he would never go to see another Bogart movie.

In a hotel in Tunis, Bogey became involved in a bar-room brawl which resulted in a good deal of damage to mirrors, walls, and furniture. Almost as soon as the fighting had petered out German bombers droned overhead, and during the raid that followed a bomb blast completed the damage which the brawl had started. Bogart was staggered when the hotel management sent him the bill for the entire damage.

At three o'clock one morning the occupants of an Italian hotel came tumbling from their beds as doors banged and shouts and cries reverberated along the corridors. An enemy attack seemed imminent. But the noise and excitement proved to have been caused by an enraged Bogart crashing along banging on doors in his search for a fellow U.S.O. entertainer, former world heavyweight champion Jack Sharkey. The ex-champ, who had also been a Navy man, had done or said something to upset Bogart, who yelled at the top of his voice that he intended to beat the ex-prize fighter from a jelly to a pulp. For once Bogart's ally instead of his adversary, Mayo was close on his heels shrieking that she was going to pulverize any portion of Sharkey that her partner might leave out.

Peter Lorre, the sinister actor with the protruding eyes, was also on the tour and forecast that Bogey and Mayo would be thrown out of Africa for fighting. But no such drastic action had to be taken, and when the tour ended the Battling Bogarts headed back to the U.S.A., leaving the military organizers of the tour heaving vast sighs of relief and happy to be able to get on with the war "in peace".

Back at home the battlers resumed battle. Then on October 19, 1944, Bogart moved out and announced to the Press that he had left Sluggy at home. She was not available for comment, but the inevitable stories about what had caused the final rift soon began to trickle through the grapevine. It had been a quarrel over politics: Mayo was a rabid Dewey supporter while Bogart was all for Roosevelt. It was woman trouble: Bogart was always taunting Mayo with some woman or other, and they were always better looking than her and a good deal cleverer. Bogart was big box office, while Mayo was small-time and way out of his league. Whatever. The columnists and muckrakers had a ball.

In later years, Mayo recalled that she and Bogart had fallen in love while working together at Warner Brothers on *Masked Woman*, in which Bette Davis had starred. She said that thereafter she had always kept a wary eye on the effect his leading ladies had on Bogart, but she had certainly underestimated the tall, slender girl cast opposite him in *To Have and Have Not*. That girl was Betty Joan Peske, whose screen name was Lauren Bacall.

Mayo had seen some of the rushes of love scenes between Bogey and Bacall in the new film and was not happy about what she saw. The acting, for her money, was not acting. She said, "I've seen Bogey make love on the screen before, but it was never like that. That was for real."

Bogey first met Betty Peske in the office of Howard Hawks, the famous producer-director of *To Have and Have Not* and *The Big Sleep*. She was a nineteen-year-old tawny blonde from the Bronx. No startling beauty by Hollywood standards, she was tall, long-legged, and somewhat angular, but her feline appearance was striking and Bogey took to her at once. He was twenty-five years older than Betty, but as rumours of the new romance spread, Bogart fans were hardly

surprised, having seen Bogart the villain revealed as a romantic personality in love scenes with Ingrid Bergman in *Casablanca*.

To Have and Have Not was released in January 1945 to rave reviews, and Warner executives were cock-a-hoop. In Lauren Bacall they had acquired a new star described as a combination of Katharine Hepburn, Marlene Dietrich, Tallulah Bankhead and Bette Davis with dabs here and there of Barbara Stanwyck, Veronica Lake, Mae West, and Jean Harlow for good measure. That was a publicity build-up that was going to be hard to live up to.

Columnists professed to be enraptured by her husky voice, by her "long-lashed" look, whatever that was supposed to mean, and by her slinky, sexy movements, Louis Sobol wrote at the time: "The real treat is a beautiful sexy newcomer named Lauren Bacall – the most exciting film girl to come along since Marlene Dietrich first thrilled us in *The Blue Angel*."

That was the girl whom Bogart fell in love with at first sight. That was the girl he knew he wanted for the rest of his life. His marriage with Mayo was all over bar the shouting, but with the legal formalities still pending Warner were alarmed when Bogey openly professed his love for their new star. The studio wired him in New York in an effort to muzzle him, saying he was hurting the dignity of Warner Brothers.

Bogart's succinct reply was typical. He wired Warner: "Do you want me to come to the coast to handle Errol Flynn's publicity? Regards, Bogart." (Errol's love life and escapades were a constant source of spicy copy for gossip writers and scandalmongers.)

On May 10, 1945, Mayo and Bogart were divorced and Bogey married Betty Peske. They stayed together until he died in January 1957. It was a happy marriage.

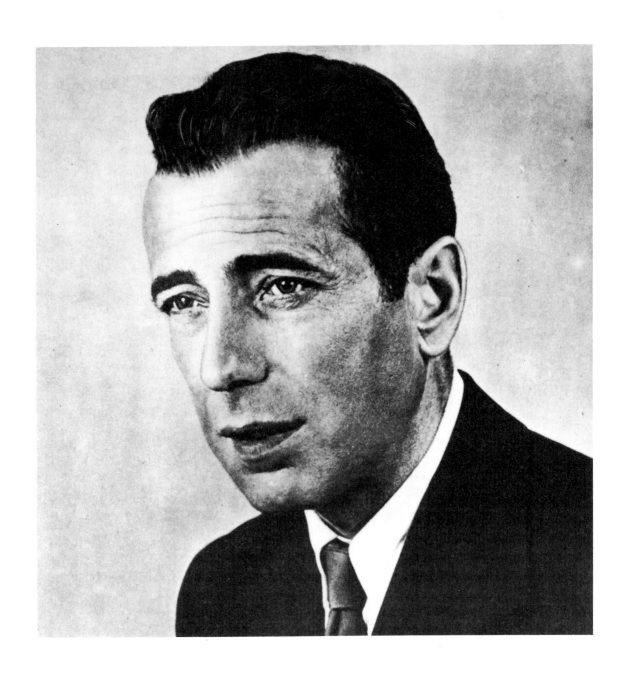